"The Meeting of the Union on New Hall Hill." Painting by B. R. Haydon.

THE BIRMINGHAM POLITICAL UNION

and the Movements for Reform in Britain.

1830-1839

The

Birmingham Political

Union

and the

Movements for Reform in Britain

1830-1839

BY

CARLOS FLICK

Archon Books

Dawson

© 1978 by Carlos Flick

First published in 1978

Archon Books, The Shoe String Press Inc
995 Sherman Avenue, Hamden, Connecticut 06514 USA

Wm Dawson & Sons Ltd, Cannon House
Folkestone, Kent, England

Archon ISBN 0-208-01752-6
Dawson ISBN 0 7129 0838 2

Printed in the United States of America

Library of Congress Cataloging in Publication Data

Flick, Carlos, 1927-
The Birmingham Political Union
and the movements for reform in Britain, 1830-1839.

Bibliography: p.
Includes index.
1. Great Britain. Parliament—Reform—History.
2. Great Britain—Politics and government—1830-1837.
3. Chartism. 4. Birmingham Political Union. I. Title.
JN543.F58   322.4'4'0941   78-14732

Contents

6

ILLUSTRATIONS

"The Meeting of the Union on New Hall Hill," painting by
B. R. Haydon, Courtesy the Birmingham Art Gallery.
frontispiece

page 91

THOMAS ATTWOOD. From the frontispiece in C. M. Wakefield,
Life of Thomas Attwood (London, 1885). The picture is
from a painting by G. Sharples, engraved and published in London, July 10, 1832.

JOSHUA SCHOLEFIELD. Sketch by B. R. Haydon. Courtesy the
City of Birmingham Museums and Art Gallery.

THOMAS C. SALT. From *The Charter*, March 3, 1839, page 1.
By permission of the British Library.

page 92

GEORGE F. MUNTZ. From the *Illustrated London News*, March
24, 1849, page 196. By permission of the British
Library.

GEORGE EDMONDS. From a drawing on page 354, vol. II of
Robert K. Dent, *Old and New Birmingham* (3 vols.,
Birmingham, 1879-1880).

DR. ARTHUR WADE. Sketch by B. R. Haydon. Courtesy the
City of Birmingham Museums and Art Gallery.

Acknowledgments

It is with pleasure that I record my gratitude to numerous persons who aided me in the research and writing of this work on the Birmingham Political Union. I am much indebted to Miss Dorothy McCulla and the staff of the Birmingham Reference Library for their unfailing courtesy and assistance during my many visits to the library over a period of several summers. Mrs. Geoffrey Williams permitted me to use the Wakefield MSS in her possession and was a most gracious hostess. Others to whom I owe my thanks for permission to examine manuscripts are Mr. F. D. Muntz, Mr. J. E. Fagg and the Dean and Warden of the Durham Colleges, the Rt. Hon. Earl Spencer, the Rt. Hon. Viscount Lambton, Sir Fergus Graham, and Mr. Joseph W. Scott, Librarian of the University College, London. Closer home, Professors Henry Warnock and John Cell read the entire manuscript and gave helpful advice (the faults which persist of course are my own failing). Miss Bessie Killebrew patiently endured innumerable revisions in typing the manuscript. Mr. Dumont Bunn was of much assistance in securing books through interlibrary loans. Finally, I am grateful to Mercer University and to the American Philosophical Society for grants which supported the project.

Introduction

THE BIRMINGHAM POLITICAL UNION figured prominently in the agitation for electoral changes in Britain during the 1830s, being involved both in the drive for the great reform bill of 1832 and in the growth of Chartism. The nature and extent of the union's contribution to each movement, however, requires reexamination, for the facts do not agree with the received tradition. This study seeks to present the union's correct place in the events of the period.

Debate among historians over the politics of the reform decades inevitably has focused on the reasons for the introduction and passage of the reform bill and on its aftereffects. The first and major interpreters of the subject were the Whig (now "traditional") school of historians. They insisted that it was the foresight and ability of the Whig party which envisioned the reform measure and accomplished its passage. The groundwork for this interpretation was laid by the patriarch of the school, Thomas Babington Macaulay, but the chief work of erecting it for modern scholarship was performed by J. R. M. Butler in *The Passing of the Great Reform Bill* (London, 1914) and by G. M. Trevelyan in *Lord Grey of the Reform Bill* (London, 1920). Both men believed that the Whigs responded to a unified, urban, middle-class agitation for the reform bill and both concluded that the Grey ministry saved Britain from revolution by timely concessions to this insurgent sector of society. The continuing persuasiveness of this approach is evidenced by the best full-scale study of the passage of the bill to appear since Butler's book, Michael Brock's *Great Reform Act* (London, 1973). Brock cited most of the detailed work performed by scholars during the past fifty years and acknowledged the contributions of revisionists, but he did not alter the grand design of Trevelyan and Butler.

Yet the Whig interpretation was narrow in that it limited its attention largely to the exploits of Whig aristocrats and urban liberals. Numerous revisionists in recent years have denounced this exclusiveness. As a result of their efforts scholarly opinion now generally dictates that space be provided for the presence and participation of other groups in the movement for reform, even if on a limited scale.

Among these groups, there is no question but that the landed interests, particularly the Whiggish portion, were active in promoting and carrying parliamentary reform, and that they were probably equal in influence to the urban population. Contemporary newspaper accounts, for example, generally gave more space to the county meetings than to the town ones. The Whig politicians themselves recognized fully the importance of the rural agitators, but historians of the Whig school later minimized their participation in favor of that of the urban reformers, perhaps because of the subsequent association of rural interests with Conservatism. Nevertheless, were the rural Tories without influence in the coming and carrying of parliamentary reform? Historians such as Norman Gash (*Politics in the Age of Peel* [London, 1953] and *Reaction and Reconstruction in English Politics, 1832–1852* [London, 1954]), G. Kitson Clark (*The Making of Victorian England* [London, 1962]), and D. C. Moore (*The Politics of Deference* [New York, 1976]) specifically have protested the downgrading of the role of the Tory agriculturalists in the reform bill period. By way of refutation, however, they have cited mainly circumstantial evidence such as concessions given to the rural interests by the bill and the undiminished power of the gentry and aristocracy in the postreform era; there is as yet no detailed account of the rural agitation itself.

Not all revisionists are conservatives, of course, and a sizable collection of historians whose sentiments and subjects lie to the left of the Whig school have published their views. The strongest of the "left" groups in terms of professorial adherents have been the Philosophical Radicals, or Benthamites. Unlike the Tories, the Philosophical Radicals unquestionably favored parliamentary reform, and Elie Halévy early sponsored their claim to a role in the passage of the bill. Traditional historians accordingly have awarded them some space, but far less than their advocates wish. The difficult task of the partisans of the Philosophical Radicals has been to show that the group's talk of political strategies and wirepulling decisively influenced the growth of agitation and the decisions of the party leaders. Joseph Hamburger attempted to overcome this obstacle in his *James Mill and the Art of Revolution* (New Haven, 1963) by showing that the reform crisis was a hoax successfully perpetrated by the followers of Mill and Bentham in order to frighten the Whigs. Subsequently R. S. Neale offered a different solution (*Class and Ideology in the Nineteenth Century* [London, 1972]) by advancing a "five-class model" in which a "middling class" of professional men, petit bourgeoisie, literate artisans, and others could act as a separate stratum suitable for the preachments of Mill, Bentham, and likeminded political philosophers.

Farther to the left in the historical spectrum have been historians sympathetic to the working classes, represented best in early years by Fabian writers such as Sidney and Beatrice Webb, J. L. and Barbara Hammond, and G. D. H. Cole. There was little conflict between them and the Whig historians because both schools agreed that the workingmen at the time of the reform bill were largely nonpolitical. It was this discrimination by both schools that E. P. Thompson proposed to correct in his *Making of the English Working Class* (London, 1963). Thompson sought to endow the working classes with an independent political identity and role by giving them a consciousness based on ideology and large-scale subversive activity rather than just ascribing to them social and economic sensibilities. This theme has since been advanced by John Foster (*Class Struggle and the Industrial Revolution* [New York, 1974]), who found that the class consciousness fostered a political split between the skilled and unskilled workers. But neither Thompson nor Foster examined the agitation for parliamentary reform.

All of these competing interpretations have in common the failure to go into the country and study the agitation at close hand, although the conjectures seem to necessitate it. As early as 1952 Asa Briggs demonstrated the value of such an approach ("The Background of the Parliamentary Reform Movement in Three

English Cities [1830–1832]," *Cambridge Historical Journal*, X, 3 [1952]), but it has not been followed up. The historians of the various national groups, both parties and classes, assumed that their subjects acted cohesively on a regional and national scale, making local distinctions relatively unimportant. Yet there has been little evidence advanced to support this supposition with respect to the reform agitation, and in its absence the role of the Birmingham Political Union has loomed large. To the degree that the chosen subjects fail to explain the movement of events, the union has served as a backup, acting as a vague but omnipresent organizer of nationwide agitation for the reform bill. Although the idea of a national influence exerted by the union is based largely upon claims advanced by the leaders of the society themselves, their importance has been unquestioned. Indeed, in many accounts Thomas Attwood, the founder of the union, is depicted as a virtual monarch during the reform era.

The evidence presented in this study does not uphold the accepted view, either of directed, unified action by classes and parties in behalf of parliamentary reform, or of an overriding influence upon the agitation by the Birmingham union. The experience of Birmingham suggests that the reform movement in the industrial towns of Britain actually had little central direction from anybody and involved almost no coordination of activity with reformers in other places. Although political parties identified ideologically with national leaders and issues, their main focus was upon problems and contentions of the immediate area. Classes and class-consciousness also existed, and the above parties reflected them, but they fitted into the mold of local economic and social relationships. In each of the industrial towns there was a peculiar mix of local traditions, factional alliances, and class connections which made its politics distinct. Thus, as Professor Briggs has pointed out, the movement in Birmingham for the reform bill had more of a provincial character than a national one.

The Birmingham Political Union was a local creation and it never transcended its provincial origins and character. In 1830 when the movement for parliamentary reform was getting underway in Britain, the union was achieving power in Birmingham through an alliance between the Ultra-Tories and Radicals and through the use of doctrines and pageantry which had strong local appeal. The union thereby attracted the shopkeepers and workers to its fold. But when its leaders attempted to reach and direct the middle and working classes nationally through the London press and through other unions, they failed. It was an ironic failure, nevertheless, for the very provincialism which had made the union so successful in its limited sphere now helped to foster a myth in the Midlands that the union acting alone by moral action had engaged distant oligarchs and had generated the movement in Britain for parliamentary reform.

This fiction in turn permitted the leaders of the union to remain relatively inactive during most of the agitation for the reform bill introduced by the Whig government, but simultaneously to imagine that they commanded the entire movement in the nation by periodic declarations of principles. When they bestirred themselves directly into the agitation, Attwood and his associates were more concerned to curtail radical activity than to spur further reformist action. The major exception to this hesitancy were the two great regional meetings for reform sponsored by the union, meetings in which unions from the surrounding area participated and which were made possible by conditions unique to Birmingham at the time. These meetings inflated the illusion of moral power exercised by the union, and led the council of the society to suppose that they themselves were primarily responsible for the passage of the reform bill. Theirs was a local triumph, in short, which through the peculiar lens of provincial conditions got magnified into national pretensions.

Meanwhile, most of the parties and classes to which historians have assigned major roles in the period were active in Birmingham, yet few of them fitted the patterns ascribed to them in these accounts. There was an obvious class consciousness present among the workers, for example, but no evidence of working-class regional or national political coordination in the agitation for parliamentary reform. Philosophical Radicals in Birmingham were limited to Joseph Parkes and a few friends, and the idea that they appealed to some special sub-class or that they decisively influenced the union or participated in a great deception is not sustained by the evidence. Nor did the Radicals of the Painite tradition fit into a larger picture. Likewise, the Ultra-Tories who led the union had almost no contact with members of that party outside of Birmingham, rural or urban. As for the Whigs and Tories of the city, they acted without close contacts with the national leaders of their parties, there being no need for elaborate electoral organizations in the unrepresented towns. Even the Birmingham Political Union had little communication with other unions outside of the immediate area. Thus Birmingham was part of a larger movement, but to a surprising degree it was a self-contained part of it.

When the leaders of the union attempted to apply their "moral power" to new demands after the passage of the reform bill, their claims of national leadership collapsed. The country ignored them and the shopkeepers of Birmingham deserted them. Party politics now exerted a growing pull within the newly enfranchised industrial towns, and the unionists could not escape involvement with the Birmingham Whigs and Dissenters in their struggles against the town's Conservatives. Yet such participation was dissatisfying, if not demeaning, to men who believed that they once had led the entire nation, and so the return of economic distress to Britain in 1837 brought a revival of the Birmingham union. The union soon was involved in the movement that would be known as Chartism, and it continued its participation until the Convention met in 1839. Historians thus have had to consider the society's contribution to that movement as well, although the question has received far less attention than has the union's part in the earlier agitation.

The original historians of the Chartist movement were the Fabians, who now have become the "traditional" school of interpretation. Mark Hovell's *The Chartist Movement* (New York, 1918) long remained the definitive study of the subject, and his main conclusions in fact are reaffirmed by J. T. Ward's recent book, *Chartism* (New York, 1973). In these accounts the lead role in organizing the Chartist drive was assigned to the London Working Men's Association, with lesser attention being given to the radicals of northern England. The Birmingham union was conceded only a minor part in the drama. In addition to the regional studies now appearing, revisionists have arisen in recent years, both to the right and to the left of the traditional school. Writers on one side such as D. J. Rowe ("The London Working

Men's Association and the 'People's Charter'," *Past and Present*, 36 [April 1967]) and Brian Harrison and Patricia Hollis ("Chartism, Liberalism, and the Life of Robert Lowery," *English Historical Review*, LXXXII, 324 [1967]) have argued for greater Philosophical Radical and Liberal emphases in dealing with the Chartists of London and the North, and new left historians such as E. J. Hobsbawm and E. P. Thompson on the other side have contended for a greater importance for an indigenous, revolutionary leadership within the working classes. Neither side, however, has concerned itself much with Birmingham and the Birmingham union, leaving the city and the organization to their reform bill laurels.

The Birmingham union, nevertheless, had a larger part in the development of Chartism than has been acknowledged. The council of the union were principally instrumental in organizing the movement for political democracy in the late 1830s, and they did so on the basis of their continued belief in the efficacy of moral action. Their strategy for the movement called for them to mobilize the workers nationally in a moral agitation that would effectively use the numerical strength of the working classes, thereby replacing the council's old program of proclamations addressed to innumerable independent meetings of local reformers. The key elements in the new drive were plans for a national petition and a national convention, tactical devices through which the council hoped to overcome both the localism and the emerging party politics which had restricted their hand in the preceding period. The leaders of the union found, however, that these larger tactics also compelled them to revamp the old myth which had sustained them in the drive for the reform bill. They now had to divorce the legend from the peculiar conditions at Birmingham which had spawned and nurtured it, a change soon reflected in the muted level of their apocalyptic and utopian pronouncements. Gone or diminished was the idea of a chosen city acting in the name of an ancient unity of classes and engaging evil monetary, boroughmongering conspirators in a great moral confrontation which would at once inaugurate a new age of prosperity and harmony. The fresh drive consisted instead of an expedient appeal to a single class on the basis of a political democracy in which the Ultra-Tory leaders of the union did not

15

genuinely believe, but one which they hoped somehow might lead eventually to monetary changes. The plan of agitation was clear enough, but the enemy and the reasons for engaging him had become even vaguer than before.

When the council initiated their campaign, they found themselves inadequate to the task. They then had no choice but to ally with radicals who scoffed at the unionist myth and who regarded moral action only as a first step to alternative strategies. The old legend thus suffered further erosion, and all in a vain cause, for a large-scale movement upon the plan developed by the Birmingham union never gathered any momentum, in the Midlands or elsewhere. The collapse of moral action opened the door to "physical force" as advocated by Feargus O'Connor and his followers, a movement that appealed directly to the class consciousness of the workers and to which the leaders of the union strongly objected. Its appeal was such that the more violent workers of Birmingham deserted the union for it. Subsequently this alternative national strategy also collapsed, however, and Chartism continued fitfully for several years under the influence of local traditions and alliances, a medley of local activities studied effectively by Asa Briggs and others. But by now the Birmingham union was dead, not to be revived again.

Because of the distinctive political life and traditions of Birmingham in the first half of the nineteenth century, the influence of the Birmingham union upon the movements for the reform bill and for Chartism are the reverse of the interpretations traditionally given. Local conditions fostered a legend by the union that it had superintended the national agitation for the reform bill, and the belief in this myth later prompted the chieftains of the society to take the lead in organizing a national drive for political democracy. The movement for the reform bill carried all before it without much help from the union, and the campaign for democracy never got going despite the strong influence and exertions of the organization. In dealing with the Birmingham Political Union, therefore, success and failure seem relevant mostly to Birmingham itself, as, indeed, does almost all of the town's political life during this period.

CHAPTER I

The Formation of the Union

THE BIRMINGHAM POLITICAL UNION was born in the vote of a public meeting held at Beardsworth's Horse and Carriage Repository on a wintry afternoon, January 25, 1830. The venture was launched by Thomas Attwood and the High-Tory currency faction of Birmingham to carry their crusade for paper money and parliamentary reform beyond the local arena into the distant provinces of national politics. They chose this particular time to move, they later explained, because they were filled with compassion for the suffering of Englishmen during the economic recession of 1828–1829, and they were inspired by the example of the Catholic Association of Ireland, which had just won a repeal of the electoral laws discriminating against Catholics. All of the evidence substantiates these explanations. The economic distress had led Thomas Attwood and the High-Tories of Birmingham to organize a public meeting in May 1829 to petition Parliament for paper currency as a principal means of relief. Although most of the Whig and regular Tory leaders of the town boycotted that meeting, Attwood and his followers pronounced the enterprise a success and they subsequently believed that it had had an important effect throughout England. Unquestionably this notion of a national influence deriving from a purely local meeting encouraged the organizers of the event to consider further political agitation.

During the meeting Attwood had raised the question of how to obtain the change in monetary policy which he advocated, and he answered confidently, "Union—such as the Irish exhibited." If the middle and lower classes of England were organized for the first time in history into a unified political force, he theorized, beginning in Birmingham, where some sense of solidarity already existed, and then spreading elsewhere, with all of the participants contributing to a fund similar to the Catholic rent and resolutely staying within the bounds of legality, then such a union should command success, as it had for the Catholics. The distress was now sufficient, he believed, to unite these classes under the leadership of a dynamic political society.

Soon after the meeting Attwood began to look about for assistance in organizing his projected society. The first people to be enlisted were the five most outspoken local advocates of cheap money: Charles Jones, Thomas C. Salt, and Benjamin Hadley initially, and then George F. Muntz and Joshua Scholefield.[1] All but Muntz had participated in the May meeting, and, with the exception of Scholefield, who also had Whig connections, all were confirmed High Tories in politics. This combination of Ultra-Toryism and a preoccupation with the currency, together with limited wealth and education, had tended to make the six men "outsiders" in Birmingham politics, regarded with suspicion and ridicule by Whig and regular Tory leaders alike. And the sneering seemed perfectly safe: who could have imagined that nonentities such as these Ultra-Tories, augmented by only a few additions to their number, were soon to become and for almost a decade were to remain the most powerful political force in the Midlands?

From the start Attwood was the unquestioned leader of the group. A banker in his late forties, he regarded himself as an economic and political prophet and he exhibited the odd combination of talent and eccentricities which one might expect from such a figure. Both his knowledge and his interest hardly extended beyond questions of the currency, but on this intricate subject he was exceedingly well informed. More important, he believed abundant bank notes to be the sole solution to the major problems of society. Hard money was the *"master-evil,"* he said, having "caused more positive misery in England during the last seventeen years, than all the legislative acts of seven hundred years have occasioned before."[2] Other issues, be they disestablishment, Ireland, free trade, poor laws, taxes, or parliamentary reform, were viewed by Attwood as comparatively trivial, and consequently his political record was one of relative inactivity on the major questions of the time. In a series of speeches and writings he repeatedly had predicted imminent doom and destruction for the country as a result of monetary fluctuations and he untiringly had castigated the alleged manipulators of the monetary system, the "Jews" of "Change Alley," evil and cunning men whom he held exclusively responsible for the dreadful situation.

Gradually through the years Attwood had acquired some of the attributes of the effective crusader. Although he was undistinguished in appearance, with an angular face, wiry hair, dark complexion, and somber eyes, he developed a remarkable mobility of expression in his features which imparted great earnestness to his words. His voice was gruff and unpolished and was distorted by a broad provincial accent (which later caused much laughter in the House of Commons), and he used only the slightest gestures; still, he spoke with ease and with utter sincerity of purpose. He believed himself called to the great mission of saving the country, and he succeeded in convincing the Birmingham shopkeepers and workers that this was so. Even the great coat with its fur collar, which he wore in summer and winter alike, came to be a trademark and an asset to his career. His private character was never seriously questioned, and his mild temperament and gentlemanly behavior in public made him seem anything but a demagogue. In short, he was a highly unusual man, in many ways unattractive and yet somehow possessing the magnetism of a popular leader.

Next to Attwood in the official leadership of the union was Joshua Scholefield. Aged fifty-six, he was the wealthiest and among the least talented of the organizers of the society. A very small, rotund man, ruddy-complexioned, balding and bespectacled, he looked the stereotype of an office clerk; perhaps because of the weakness of his voice, he was reluctant to speak at public meetings. His education and temperament seemingly suited him for the details of business and not for public affairs. But he was moderately successful as a merchant, banker, and manufacturer, and he was highly respected in all circles of the community;

equally important, he was, despite his standing among the orthodox politicians, "currency mad" on the question of paper money.[3] He thus could bring a degree of financial support and respectability to the agitation which none of the other leaders could offer and these leaders greatly valued his association with them.

Charles Jones was a close friend and admirer of Attwood as the true prophet. For fifteen years Jones had written and spoken zealously in behalf of cheap money policies. He had a pleasing voice and appearance, but he was not a good speaker or tactician. His attacks on his opponents were always intemperate, and he perpetually was embroiled in controversy with local defenders of the "hook-nosed Jews" and "beastly Whigs" behind the policies he opposed. As one of his critics pointed out, it seemed as if Jones's trade as a silversmith and medalist was so uncreditable to him that he had to prove himself outside of his shop. But despite his shortcomings his dedication to the cause was to make him a useful member of the council of the union.

The lamp manufacturer Thomas Clutton Salt also was frequently involved in contentions, although he was much less aggressive in temperament than was Jones. His encounters usually arose from the fact that his public conduct was, in the words of a critic, "characterized by great enthusiasm but little discretion." Daniel O'Connell scathingly referred to him as "a pickled youth."[4] Now thirty-nine years old, he was of medium build and had what his contemporaries described as a very expressive face, with a large forehead, eyes, and mouth, and yet, withal, well proportioned features. His debut as a political leader came in 1826 when he led a protest in Birmingham against the government's program of "fiscal oppression." He was widely regarded as a good-hearted man, and his espousal of the causes of the lower classes seemingly was more genuine than was that of the other "currency" leaders, whose bent was aristocratic. He was loquacious, and although his voice was thin and his reasoning often poor, he spoke at every opportunity. Like Jones, he accepted Attwood's economic views as the final word in politics: "That gentleman had . . . said, that the scourge inflicted upon the earth by the barbarous Attila, would not equal the scourge which he foretold. Who could deny that the prediction had been accomplished?"[5]

The least known of the men whom Attwood first recruited was Benjamin Hadley. He was born on July 14, 1791, a day of liberty, of which he liked to remind his friends. A manufacturer of pearl buttons, he, like Jones, seemingly needed the excitement of popular movements to escape the monotony of the shop. His style of speaking was little short of frenzied: a Tory opponent called him "an inflated and stilted Demosthenes," and a Whig after hearing him speak declared that he had never heard such language or seen such extraordinary gestures used. Reportedly Hadley was a handsome man, but no picture or description of him is extant. His Dissenting background accorded well with what was generally described as a stern and inflexible character. While he agreed wholeheartedly with Attwood's economic philosophy, he did not consider himself competent to expound publicly on the subject of the currency, making that topic one of the very few on which he remained relatively silent.

George Frederick Muntz evidently was the last of the Ultra-Tory spokesmen to be enlisted in the new project. He had not participated in the May meeting, but he had signed the requisition for it and he recently had spoken and written in favor of paper money. The first of his three *Letters to the Duke of Wellington* on the subject of distress and bank notes was written only a few days before the meeting.[6] Muntz thus shared with the others an acceptance of Attwood's views on economics, but in other respects he was much more his own man. He was the youngest of the six initial leaders and undoubtedly the most enterprising. Born in 1794, he took over the management of his father's metal-rolling mill in 1811 and realized a modest income from it until 1832, when his discovery of a new alloy opened the way to the gradual acquisition of a small fortune.[7] In appearance he was most unusual: he was very heavy and muscular, and in a day when shaving was almost universal he sported a bushy black beard. In his faded blue coat and baggy trousers, with an outsized walking stick in his hand and with a noticeable swagger to his gait, he was an unmistakable figure in Birmingham. His manners were coarse and his temper was short. His policy for dealing with enemies, he said, was the direct blow in the face. He was fluent, and his powerful voice and rough-and-ready oratory were to make him a favorite speaker at the union rallies. Perhaps some of his eccentricities were affected, for, as one observer noted, he seemed to crave notoriety. He maintained that he was a republican "in principle," yet all of his sentiments were staunchly monarchical. His talents and aggressiveness were to make him the logical successor to Attwood as chairman in 1833, but his lack of finesse and caution was also to raise difficulties for the union.

All five of these men of course were already in Attwood's political camp. The banker's real task was to find support for his proposed society from outside the High-Tory currency faction. The enterprise was not an easy one. Birmingham's political life, like that of most of the provincial industrial towns, was loosely organized about a spectrum of unstructured local parties. (The city differed from other large towns only in that other places had a different assortment of parties and arrangements.) The city's parties shared general political traditions with like-minded groups elsewhere in the nation, but the focus of their appeals, activities, and alliances was on Birmingham itself. Attwood's Ultra-Tory faction appealed mainly to the marginal merchants and manufacturers in Birmingham who had felt the squeeze of a fluctuating economy and who could be persuaded that a scarcity of money was the sole cause of their troubles. Because small, diversified workshops were relatively numerous in Birmingham, there was a larger audience for Attwood's views than was found in other major industrial towns, a fact that made the banker's currency party a novelty in the eyes of political observers elsewhere.[8] Even so, the faction remained small in size. Like many Ultra-Tories in other parts of the country, Attwood's group justified its stances by citing ancient political traditions of England, a source of political identity that antedated the seventeenth- and eighteenth-century origins of the Tory and Whig landed and commercial oligarchy. The natural constituency of the English Ultra-Tories were those groups who seemed least adapted to changing political and economic forces; yet most Ultras elsewhere were agriculturally oriented and Attwood's band had little occasion for communication and concert with them. The banker needed local allies. Where to turn?

The Birmingham Whigs and Tories were not good prospects because they expressly identified with the national parties and the traditions of each. The local situation differed from most other cities in that the Whigs of Birmingham were allied with the spokesmen for the Dissenters, a group that stressed its own seventeenth-century political and religious heritage. All three parties mainly contained upper-middle class manufacturing, commercial, and professional people, collectively constituting the principal wealth and influence of Birmingham. Their political limitation was that the city had no seats in Parliament and no accompanying large-scale patronage, and so their contacts with the national leaders were minimal. Like the Ultra-Tories whom they scorned, their base of power had to be essentially local.

To the left of these parties in the political spectrum were various radical factions. Their natural followers were the lower strata of society, growing rapidly in the industrial towns. The political leaders who termed themselves "Radical" (written with upper case) sought to speak for the shopkeepers and more "respectable" workers and were willing on occasion to cooperate with the "established" parties. A few persons—Joseph Parkes and several friends—regarded themselves as Utilitarians. Most of the group, however, talked in terms of the older radical tradition associated with Tom Paine and other agitators of the preceding century. The Radicals had been active in previous agitation for parliamentary reform and potentially were a powerful force in Birmingham life. Their potential appeared to be limited to the city, however, for they had few organized contacts with Radicals elsewhere. (The main exception was Parkes, who regularly communicated with Francis Place in London.) More aggressive than these Radicals, but very few in number, were the "radicals" (written with lower case), who advocated the cause of the working classes exclusively and who appealed not to some political tradition but directly to the emerging class consciousness of the workers. Because of the relative conservatism of the Birmingham workers, they found a smaller following than existed in places such as Manchester and Leeds; indeed, the leaders generally were spokesmen sporadically thrown up from the ranks of the shopkeepers and workers, although several of the more demagogic Radicals came forward to lead at favorable times. The absence of a fixed leadership made the more dissatisfied and hostile workers a ready audience of the demagogues from outside who sometimes visited the city or who published addresses to them. Ironically, therefore, these most disorganized of the local groups were the most ready participants in politics of a regional and national scope.

In his quest for allies Attwood had no success at first. The orthodox Tory leaders had to be written off; of their number, only Attwood's banking partner had signed the requisition for the May meeting, and even he now fell away. There is some evidence that Attwood and his lieutenants considered the alternative of recruiting allies from the distressed farmers of the area, men normally led by the Whigs and Tories of the county. About a fortnight after the May meeting, several of the Ultra-Tory faction issued a handbill calling a meeting of the agriculturalists who attended the Birmingham market. Presumably, commented one observer, "the 'lords of the soil' were to be schooled and receive *lessons* on the currency question."[9] But only a few persons showed up and the meeting was cancelled. Neither at that point nor later did the discontented farmers of the region show any interest in political cooperation with the laborers and shopkeepers of Birmingham.

Attwood was equally unsuccessful with the Whig-Dissenter party within the town. Several of the spokesmen for this group had signed the requisition for the meeting in May, probably because they hoped that the agitation over economic distress would prove embarrassing to the Duke of Wellington's government. The Ultra-Tories misread this assistance as a willingness of the party to undertake further joint action. In July, Attwood approached two of its leaders and proposed that they join him in establishing the contemplated political organization. But both men rejected the offer.[10] Others of the party meanwhile were busy ridiculing reports that Attwood and his friends had become converts to parliamentary reform and therefore acceptable partners to reformers.[11] In the end the Whig and Dissenter spokesmen almost to a man shunned any connection with the union.

Only the Radicals remained as potential allies. The way to a possible coalition between the Ultra-Tories and these former political enemies had been opened by Attwood's speech at the May meeting. He had now become a reformer, he indicated, "and a *Radical Reformer*": obviously, the events of the last fourteen years had shown that something was wrong with the representation of the people. But he added that the question "was trifling" as compared to the monetary one and that currency measures and prosperity must come first. Excited minds were not fit to agitate, he said, and he would not "wade to reform through an ocean of blood and tears." It was hardly a call to action on the subject, and he clearly had intended that his projected society agitate primarily for paper money. But by August he had changed his mind and was ready to give parliamentary reform top billing.[12] Undoubtedly one reason for the decision was the banker's pressing need for the Radicals as allies. Perhaps equally important, the Duke of Wellington and others had joined Sir Robert Peel in attacking the petition for monetary change sent to Parliament by the participants of the May meeting, and Attwood had to concede that the legislature as then constituted was unresponsive to agitation for more bank notes. The result was that the project for a political union suddenly moved in a different and highly important direction.

To confederate with the Radicals of Birmingham meant in practice that Attwood had to gain the cooperation of the three men who served as their chief spokesmen. The most influential and moderate of the three was George Edmonds, an attorney's clerk who had led the agitation for parliamentary reform in 1816–1819. His large, popular following resulted partly from his ability as a speaker: he combined the loud voice and violent gestures of a demagogue with a fluency and eloquence unmatched by any of the other men who were to lead the union. He also was the best educated of them, his father, a Baptist minister, having provided him with an excellent classical training. As a politician he was bold and impulsive. His features were an additional asset: he had dark, curly hair on a large head, clear, piercing eyes, and a round, well-proportioned face. He was of medium build and was forty-two years old at the time of the founding of the union. Without Edmonds's assistance Attwood probably could not have won and retained the support of the workers in the early months of the organization.[13]

The other leaders were William Pare and Joseph Russell. They were more radical than was Edmonds and they had a much smaller working-class following than he. Pare was proprietor of a tobacco shop and reading room (hence "Snuffy Pare" to his opponents) and also was secretary of the Mechanics' Institute. Although only twenty-five years of age, he headed the Owenite Co-operative movement in the area and had given lectures on Owenism in 1829 in the major cities of the North; within Birmingham itself he regularly made violent speeches in a nasal voice to the workers. Even his opponents conceded that he was a man of considerable energy and intelligence.[14] Russell, aged forty-four, was a printer and bookbinder, and a vender of radical literature. In spite of his profession, he barely was literate, a deficiency frequently evidenced in his speeches and pamphlets. Both men enhanced their reputations as dangerous agitators by openly avowing rationalist religious opinions. And both looked the part of conspirators. Pare was small, anemic, and bony-faced, and his quill-like hair stood on end and accentuated his large forehead. Russell was tall and thin and had a pock-marked face; his motley hair went uncombed. Like Pare, he wore thread-bare clothes which hung loosely on his gaunt frame—as loosely as his principles, his enemies declared. Both men were to find it difficult to live peaceably with their Ultra-Tory associates on the council of the union.

The details of how and when Attwood established contact with Edmonds and these men are not known. Russell had indicated in the May meeting that he had no objection to Attwood's monetary ideas as such, undoubtedly a response to the banker's declaration on reform, for he later was opposed to cheap currency. By August rumors circulated that Attwood was attempting to constitute his society on a radical basis. But all that can be stated with certainty is that the above leaders and two or three lesser figures signed the requisition and helped to organize the union in January, whereas none had lent his name to the endeavor of the preceding May.

The first formal step in establishing the union came on December 22 when about thirty persons gathered at the Globe Tavern to hear Attwood read a statement of the nature and rules of the proposed "Union for the Protection of Public Rights." The clauses of the constitution were discussed *seriatim* and approved.

Twenty-eight men—the bulk of the first council—then signed the document and immediately resolved themselves into a committee of arrangement, to carry its objects into effect.[15]

The next step was to arrange for a public meeting to approve of the formation of the union, and presumably also to launch its campaign for parliamentary reform. A difficulty was the weather, for the Midlands was experiencing the coldest temperatures in many years, with the canals frozen over and a heavy fall of snow holding fast to the ground. The only building large enough to accommodate the anticipated crowd, Beardsworth's Horse and Carriage Repository, had three hundred windows and a high, airy ceiling and was little better than the outdoors. Yet the committee was eager to get the union established before Parliament convened for its new session. Eventually they persuaded Beardsworth to allow them to light five large coke fires inside his building and to seal off all the entrances but the main one. A further delay occurred when the High Bailiff, who was a staunch Whig, refused to honor a requisition and summon a public meeting for the purpose of forming the political organization. But Attwood and eleven other Ultra-Tories finally called the meeting without official approval and set it for January 25.[16]

A large attendance was necessary if the formation of the union was not to be judged a fiasco. The organizers accordingly scheduled the meeting for a Monday, which was an idle day for most of the workers during hard times, and they advertised the measures taken to render the Repository comfortable, placarding the town meanwhile with a handbill urging all classes to attend.[17] On the appointed day a muster of workers and shopkeepers estimated by the committee at 12,000 to 15,000 persons crowded into the hall and galleries of the building; later the union's reports increased the figure to 20,000 "during the day." Without doubt these calculations were too high—Attwood in his speech guessed that 10,000 were present—and it is unlikely that many persons stood attentively in place for the entire six hours of speeches and business. Nevertheless, it was an impressive display of popular interest.

Nor was the nearly unanimous support given the leaders of the meeting less impressive. During the proceedings the Whig and Radical lawyers William Redfern and Joseph Parkes strongly opposed the formation of the union on the ground that its political goals were a mere varnish for an obsession with the currency. Redfern declared that with the exception of Scholefield none of Attwood's party had previously advocated parliamentary reform, and he shouted, "I tell you, I suspect the sincerity and zeal of the gentlemen who now bring forward these measures of reform." Parkes moved that the meeting petition for electoral change as an alternative to creating a union. But the remarks of both men were received with hissing and hooting and Attwood's motion to form the union carried by twenty to one, amidst loud and prolonged cheering. (A revised version said one thousand to one.)[18]

What was distinctive, in the opinion of its founders, about the political union which they were establishing? The uniqueness of the union in Attwood's view was that it proposed to combine politically the efforts of the two "industrious classes" of the nation, that is, the middle and lower, who were being exploited by evil men and who had been deceived into attacking and blaming each other for their sufferings. The direct cause of all of the wrongs of the land, the founders of the union declared, was the control of the House of Commons by several hundred selfish boroughmongers who headed the great monied interests of the country, men who manipulated the currency and other concerns for their private benefit and who used Parliament to legitimatize their schemes. (Although the monied conspirators might own estates, they were not to be identified with the majority of the landed aristocracy, who were largely exempt from the effects of the evil policies and therefore declined to act against them.) So effective was the conspiratorial activity of these oppressors that they kept the nation's industrious classes in almost continual distress and, through deception, at each other's throat; yet if the eyes of the victims should ever be opened to the real situation by a political union for common objects, the boroughmongers could be quickly and thoroughly vanquished. Indeed, if properly led the productive classes could overcome them without bloodshed by simply asserting the ancient rights of the people in a great moral confrontation with the usurpers, a contest of historical truth and right against political despoliation and wrong. For this reason Attwood insisted that all of the union's actions must be unfailingly legal and peaceful, lest by violence the agitators play into the hands of the boroughmongers, who commanded the military and judicial establishments of the country.

It should not be supposed from the broad constituency of the union that it was to be a democratic society. The High-Tory sentiments of its chief founders were perhaps most evident in its unabashedly authoritarian character. The *Rules and Regulations* approved at the January 25 meeting gave the ruling council unlimited power to act and speak for the union between annual business meetings. The only condition imposed upon the leaders was that they be "re-chosen" each July, and even this requirement was largely nullified by the absence of any provision for competitive elections. The council had the power to add to their number at any time, and a provision that they pay their own expenses was sufficient to keep the leadership safely middle-class. As for the members of the union, the *Rules and Regulations* stated that their obligation was "to obey strictly all the just and legal directions of the *Political Council*." Specifically, the members were to contribute dues of not less than a shilling per quarter and were to present themselves at the general meetings and at other times upon call.[19]

Inevitably, a number of points in the strategy of the union remained ambiguous. Parliamentary reform declaredly was the first objective of the society, but how much change in the electoral system was required to defeat the boroughmongers? The chief founders of the union were not democrats; and yet if they sought to enfranchise only a small portion of the "industrious classes" the workers in the union and their spokesmen on the council might well lose all interest in the enterprise. Furthermore, what measures was the union to advocate once this first goal was achieved? Obviously Attwood and his friends had in mind the currency in talking of the well-being of the industrious classes, but their Radical allies had no taste for this subject and undoubtedly would not swallow monetary changes without an accompanying diet of other reforms unpalatable to the Ultra-Tories.

Related to the above difficulties were unanswered questions of leadership. In their vision of a moral confrontation between the people and the boroughmongers, the leaders of the Birmingham union anticipated a movement in which a network of unions would be established throughout the country to help promote and direct the agitation for change. But were these other unions to be branches without wills and goals of their own, and would they accept such a status? And assuming that a significant part of the middle and lower classes proved hostile or indifferent, how could the Birmingham union claim to represent them? Also, most areas already had leaders of their own and it was unlikely that these men would readily step aside or submit to the guidance of the council of the Birmingham union, particularly if they had doubts about the effectiveness of moral action as preached by the council. The basic assumption of Attwood and his associates in answer to all of these problems was that economic distress had produced such a unity of mind and purpose among the "self-supporting classes" that geographical, social, economic, and personal distinctions had become unimportant. It was yet to be proved, however, that the disparate elements which Attwood and the others sought to unite could speak with one voice and that the council of the union at Birmingham could pronounce for them all.

Finally, what basis of constitutional authority was cited by the council in justifying a claim to such political power? The right of meeting and petitioning Parliament could hardly include the right to erect a rival deliberative body. Occasionally in the future the council would hint vaguely at the existence of a "popular sovereignty," but this was dangerous ground and admittedly it ill suited the political sentiments of Attwood's High-Tory faction. Instead, the council in their Report to the meeting of January 25 cited an unlimited royal sovereignty, proclaiming that "the *King's Throne* presents a *bulwark*, under which his faithful people may find a shelter from the oppressor's wrong," and suggesting that constitutionally the government and legislature still were merely the king's advisers. This being so, the activities of the council and of the union could be interpreted as nothing more than a similar form of assistance to the ruler in his ancient duty to know and satisfy the needs of his people, as legitimate as the role of ministers and legislators. That this position was completely anachronistic was no handicap to the council, for their appeal to a competing authority against the established political system was most usefully one that was legally imprecise and vaguely emotional. What better source than the throne?

The success of the union from the start was in fact due more to the emotional response which its leaders elicited from the people of Birmingham and the surrounding towns than to the specific issues which they touted. The container was more important than the contents. It is the secret of agitators that in their emotional appeals and denunciations they cut deeper and touch nerve endings not disturbed by more "sensible" leaders. Thus the primary success of the chief organizers of the union lay not in their commitment to the goal of paper money—the currency issue never came to the fore throughout the history of the union—nor to parliamentary reform, in which the Ultra-Tories had little genuine interest. Rather, the unionist chieftains' deeper appeal in Birmingham derived from certain characteristics of English local politics of that day which they almost unconsciously embodied in their attitudes and words. They themselves never fully understood their success because they never thought of themselves as agitators in the demagogic sense.

One of the underlying characteristics of local politics which the unionists exploited was a pronounced provincialism found in the new industrial towns. These towns had grown up outside of the older landed structure and the national politics based upon it. The lack of representation meant that places such as Birmingham had no express role in parliamentary politics. Nor was the dynamic economic life of the towns and their involvement in world markets the broadening influence which one might suppose, for the industrial centers tended to specialize in a few related items, such as hardware at Birmingham, and to trench their interests about these commodities. The leaders of commerce and industry in the towns had few contacts even with the neighboring gentry and aristocracy. Yet these urban centers were growing rapidly in population and wealth, and there was an incipient pride among their inhabitants which found expression in a budding cultural and intellectual life—but which as yet had no outlet in politics. It was the good fortune of Attwood and the other leaders of the union that they were unabashedly provincial, having no pretension to intimacy with statesmen and thinkers beyond the immediate area. Thus their profuse praise of their home town and their sincere appeal to the "men of Birmingham" to take the lead in guiding the rest of the nation elicited reactions which the regular party leaders, with their professed larger identities, could not duplicate.

The provincialism of the industrial towns helps to explain the obsession of Attwood and his closest followers with the question of the currency. The issue of cheap money was neither new nor limited to Birmingham: it was a complicated subject debated widely by economists and politicians. But the argument over the finer points was not Attwood's approach, although he was capable of it; the Birmingham banker instead saw the matter as a conspiracy by an economic elite in London to ruin the country for its selfish gain. He had a deep-seated suspicion of the powers centered in the capital, a form of political paranoia which had its echoes elsewhere in other campaigns against other conspiring elites. More cosmopolitan spokesmen in Birmingham might scoff at these prejudices, but the shopkeepers and workers did not. Eventually education, the franchise, and the railroad would erase this distorting localism and it would be replaced by the opposite extreme, the doctrine of national progress centered in the industrial towns. But in the 1830s the mistrust of London was strong.

These suspicions were related to another underlying characteristic of politics in many of the provincial towns: a predisposition toward vague millenarianism. The seventeenth-century dissenting tradition had not died in the country, and in places such as Birmingham, where Dissenters were numerous, it had the potential to color the fabric of local politics. The better educated leaders of Birmingham had "outgrown" the emotional religious fears and expectations of the earlier period and they little understood them. Not so Attwood and his circle. Although an Anglican, Attwood had deeply imbibed the religious traditions around him, and he accepted both their apocalyptic and utopian implications. When he applied them to politics, he got a ready response from the people of Birmingham. Thus his Biblical-like prophesies of disaster and his denunciations of wicked conspirators, so odd to many outside observers, did not seem strange at all to his local audiences. Equally important, his promises of utopian prosperity and happiness as an aftermath of the defeat of the monetary boroughmongers found receptive listeners. To accomplish all this, Birmingham need only confront the forces of wickedness with the truth. Attwood and his lieutenants had their counterparts elsewhere, of course, where the focus was upon other evildoers, but nowhere did the response exceed that given the political apostles at Birmingham.

In one important respect Birmingham was even more narrow in its political life than were the other industrial towns. Currents of larger interests were beginning to end the political isolation of the new towns, and none more strongly than a growing class consciousness on the part of both the middle and working classes. Much more than was the case at Manchester, Leeds, and other large towns, however, Birmingham remained a center of diversified workshops. Here the masters and skilled workmen labored in relatively close contact, and workers generally were better paid and housed than elsewhere. The result was a greater tolerance of each other and a relative conservatism among the working classes. The unionists' concentration upon the currency issue was itself a reflection of this apparent local amity, for attacks on the ill-gotten gains of distant financiers were not as class divisive as was agitation centering on elites whose profits controlled the price of food and the provision of relief for the poor and unemployed. Based upon the outward experience of Birmingham, Attwood was prepared to deny that there was any class antagonism in Britain as a whole. He judged matters erroneously, however, for even Birmingham was not immune to increasing differences among its inhabitants over economic and political objectives, something the union itself was to discover, beginning on the founding day.

Authorization to form the union was quickly obtained. The second task announced for the meeting of January 25 was to petition for parliamentary reform. The requisition and advance publicity implied that it was to be a major item of business. Yet the leaders of the meeting actually moved their petition at the end of the day's activity, when darkness was approaching and when few persons remained in the hall; the official *Proceedings* did not

even report it.[20] More surprising, the document they offered did
not mention parliamentary reform at all. Instead, it was a copy of
a petition for the repeal of beer and malt duties, which had been
read, but not adopted, at a meeting of the Cambridgeshire freeholders three days before. The work of a Huntingdon-based itinerant radical named Samuel Wells, the document had appeared
as part of a report of the Cambridgeshire meeting carried by the
London *Morning Chronicle* on January 23 and thus presumably
was not known to the members of the council until shortly before
the Birmingham meeting. Why, then, should they have waited
until the last moment to act upon so important a matter as the
petition, and then have adopted hastily a document whose main
object was so foreign to the announced purposes of their own
meeting?

The only plausible answer is that differences within the council
prevented agreement on a petition for parliamentary reform.
Eight additional persons had been recruited for the council by
January 25, bringing that body to the minimum of thirty-six
required by the *Rules and Regulations*. Most of its members
apparently agreed with the six original leaders in their political
opinions. Several of them were to take a fairly active part in the
council's affairs, notably John Betts, a metal refiner in his middle
fifties and, next to Scholefield, probably the wealthiest member
of the council in 1830; James W. Evans, japanner, who was to be
called "Goose Evans" by his opponents after he fainted when
hissed at at a union meeting; and Thomas Parsons, Jr., a metal
dealer. Most of the other Ultra-Tory council members were small
businessmen, and most were older than the six men who started
the organization. The difficulty for Attwood and his friends, of
course, was that the Radical leaders also found several strong
supporters within the council. Among them were the Luckcock
brothers, Felix and Urban, lime and brick dealers and sons of a
Unitarian minister and veteran reformer; they were in their early
thirties and were firm Radicals. Also, there was Josiah Emes, a
white-haired little man called "Pigmy Emes" who, despite his
age of sixty-two years, found time away from his button shop to
espouse radical causes.

It would appear that the small band of Radicals headed by
Russell, Pare, and Edmonds reached an impasse with Attwood's

party over what degree of parliamentary reform to demand. Attwood claimed in his speech at the meeting that he and his friends had always been radical reformers, only silent ones, but it was an assertion easily refuted,[21] and in fact he and his followers, while evidently genuine converts to reform, meant by the term "radical" something far from democratic. When they cited the "ancient constitution" of Saxon England, they evoked images of a period when many commoners allegedly exercised political privileges, but exercised them by the grace of the king and not through any inalienable claims of their own. The Radicals differed strongly with their fellow unionists on this matter. They talked rather of rational rights and of the natural equality of men, of doctrines fashionable since the recent revolutionary period. It was probably because of this division over reform that Jones and Hadley, both Ultra-Tories, moved the petition which in effect postponed a decision on the subject. The union's campaign for great changes was off to an uncertain start, and it remained to be seen whether the divided council of such a body could guide the national mind and redress the public wrongs of the British people.

CHAPTER II

Prelude to Parliamentary Reform

1830

ONE OF THE MISFORTUNES to befall crusaders is the discovery that much of their time must be given to camp duties rather than to engaging the enemy in the field. This sobering revelation soon came to the founders of the union, for whom the exciting business of mustering the public and overseeing the passage of resolutions of ambitious intent now gave way to routine problems of administering a fledgling political organization. The council found as well that those political forays which most readily could be undertaken were not adventuresome encounters with distant enemies, but rather were minor struggles with cantankerous, local opponents, men who were their acquaintances and neighbors.

The council's goals nevertheless went beyond the conducting of neighborhood skirmishes, and therein lay the difficulty. An organization for political agitation in the provincial cities of Britain in 1830 had almost insuperable obstacles to overcome if it aspired to genuine national influence. Many radicals in previous years had experienced these limitations. First, the provincial character of political life in the towns made local issues and activities more important than national ones. Frequently the populace would muster strong support for local concerns, but only rarely would it rouse to action on questions of national scope. Second, there existed powerful legal restrictions upon political societies, enacted by governments during former periods of agitation. The leaders of an organization could disregard the prohibitions, as many radicals chose to do, but the ministers then could jail the leaders, as ministers frequently chose to do. Finally, emerging class differences in the towns made the twin necessities of any organization for agitation—a large membership on the one hand, and men of wealth and influence on the other—difficult to achieve simultaneously. The organizers of the society usually had to forego one as the price of attracting the other.

The last obstacle was the initial one to be encountered by the founders of the union, for money and members were the first essentials of getting organized. Almost at once the council started a campaign to enlist members. Like most of the initial organizing activities, the effort was low keyed, in keeping with Attwood's expectation that the distress automatically would bring the middle and lower classes into the union's fold. The results were exceedingly modest. At a meeting in May the council reported only 2,200 men on the union's roll. Equally discouraging, those persons who joined were almost entirely workers and shopkeepers, despite reports made to the press that the union was daily receiving accessions of strength from all quarters, high and low, rich and poor. At the May meeting Attwood admitted reluctantly that the middle class (meaning the manufacturers, large merchants, and professional people, for the council considered shopkeepers to be lower class) had not come forward but he declared that it was with him in sentiment.[1] The banker later explained to his wife that the "respectable men" did not admit their interest in the union because "few have the courage to own it."[2] The best that he and his associates could do was to maintain that the union of the "industrious classes" was operative because the council spoke both for the workers and shopkeepers and for the absent but allegedly favorable upper middle class. Such declarations may have been necessary for propaganda, but it remained true that the more established middle class in Birmingham was deeply suspicious of the Ultra-Tory and Radical outsiders on the council and of the "mob" in the union, and they denied the society their contributions and support from the start.

The alternative for the council was to raise money from the rank and file membership itself, much as Daniel O'Connell had done in Ireland. In their first weekly meeting, at the Globe Tavern on February 10, 1830, the council appointed thirteen of their number who had shops or offices in various parts of town to receive the penny-a-week dues from the members. They also directed that a union office be opened at No. 1 Paradise Street to enroll members and to receive money.[3] But the futility of expecting the workers voluntarily to bring their contributions to certain offices soon was apparent. The lower classes in the town ordinarily did not contribute to "causes." The members of the union clearly expected the middle-class councilmen to take care of the finances themselves. The council consequently had to hire collectors to canvass the members for dues, an exercise that also was without much success. It was the beginning of an almost insoluble problem for the union's leaders. Attwood and his associates had expected to emulate the Catholic Association in the collection of what Attwood called "the sinews of law," but the union's campaign was not a religious one and the Birmingham workers were not Irishmen.

In the foregoing arrangements the council ignored the most obvious method of contact with the members: the establishment of branches and the appointment of sectional leaders. The principal obstacle to this form of organization was the council's authoritarian view of the union, which called for the leaders to speak for the followers without having to confer with them. There remained, nevertheless, a desire among the rank and file for comradeship between general meetings, and gradually the members began to gather at certain taverns to discuss politics. Within a year there were twenty-six of these unofficial "sectional houses." Only the Radicals on the council seemed to recognize their real value, and some of these men began cautiously to utilize them for working-class agitation of their own devising. The potential for class divisiveness thus reached deeper into the union itself.

However, among the lower classes of Birmingham the union did grow in numbers and reputation. During the following months the council almost inadvertently found the keys to favorable popular notice and increased membership within Birmingham, although their success was limited to workers and shopkeepers and brought no substantial enlargement of finances. One of the devices which they discovered was an active involvement in local issues. The other was the use of spectacle to attract attention and to generate interest in the union.

The latter activity developed around a meeting to further the council's announced intention to conduct agitation for parliamentary reform. There was, of course, a major problem in this regard: before there could be any serious activity, the leaders of the union had to agree upon the extent of the reform they desired. The Ultra-Tory majority favored a moderate plan recently presented to Parliament by Lord Blandford. Only four days after the January 25 meeting, Blandford, an Ultra-Tory who unsuccessfully had moved a resolution in 1829 condemning close boroughs, wrote Attwood of his "intense interest and satisfaction" at what had been done in Birmingham. Although a stranger to the council personally, he said, he was convinced that it was from the High-Tory quarter that reform must emanate: "I have now the pleasure to assure you, that I am prepared to introduce a Bill into the House (falsely called the Commons House) which is so constructed as to meet *every single point* you dwell on in the report of your speech."[4] Blandford accordingly presented to the Commons a plan to transfer seats from close boroughs to large towns and to establish a household suffrage; but his motion to introduce a bill on the subject was defeated. Attwood strongly favored this plan and he and the Ultra-Tories on the council continued to argue for it despite its rejection by Parliament. The Radicals, however, contended for universal suffrage, annual parliaments, and the ballot. Evidently the decisive moment in the discussion occurred when Edmonds came over to the Ultra-Tory moderate camp; on March 16 the council were able after prolonged discussion to issue unanimously a declaration to the country in favor of the Marquis of Blandford's scheme of reform. The Declaration urged that the proposed measure everywhere "be adopted as the common *rallying point* of the People."[5]

The council's next move was to call a meeting of the union to obtain from the members a formal endorsement of the Declaration. To this end they summoned a general meeting for May 17. But once more there was dissension among the leaders, as the Radicals now balked at the holding of a public meeting in which they would have to openly repudiate their democratic principles. Someone—reportedly William Pare—wrote the radical Henry Hunt in London and enlisted his help in condemning the Declaration, and Hunt responded by publishing an address to the members of the union calling upon them *"to resist and repudiate the trap that was laid for them."* The controversy was not settled until the eve of the meeting, for the advertisement which announced the event mentioned only proposed alterations in the *Rules and Regulations* and "a Report" which the council would submit.[6] But at the last moment the Radicals gave way.

Meanwhile, the council had taken steps to attract a large turnout of members and spectators for the meeting, lest a small attendance give the impression of weak backing for their leadership. The provision of spectacle was important, for most people in the drab industrial towns had few sources of diversion. Crowds gathered readily for any excitement, regardless of its purpose and sponsorship. But because the idea of "artificially" generated excitement smacked of demagoguery, the chieftains of the union only gropingly moved toward it. Some of them at first even opposed the use of a band. But eventually, at Attwood's insistence, they issued a colorful political union medal to stimulate enrollment in the union, and they planned a procession of members, replete with band and banners, through the principal streets to Beardsworth's Repository.

The result of the "display and exhibition" exceeded all of their expectations. An estimated 80,000 to 100,000 persons gathered early in the morning to participate in or to observe the march. Hundreds of men pressed into the union's rooms to enroll their names and receive the union medal. Then, preceded by the band and flanked by a sturdy bodyguard, the council led the "floating pavement of human heads" through the streets to the Repository. Although the figures on attendance there—reported at 18,000 to 20,000 persons—may have been much exaggerated, there is no doubt that the council had discovered workable techniques for producing excitement and drawing a crowd. Enrollment in the union now had doubled, to about 5,000 members.

The new members were "soft," attracted more by the novelty and excitement of the occasion than by a concern for issues. Few of them paid their dues. Yet their names were on the roll, and the growing appearance of power helped attract to the council several additional Radicals who were interested in local reforms and who saw in the union a tool to accomplish them. This involvement, in turn, further strengthened the organization.

The Radicals and others replaced by co-optation men who had been virtually inactive in the initial activities and who had resigned. Three of the Radical newcomers, William Weston, John Pierce, and Thomas Parkin, were to play prominent roles in the union. Weston was a merchant (an accountant after his business failed in 1832) who possessed a shrill voice and a strong admiration for Henry Hunt. Pierce was a thimble manufacturer who had been converted to radicalism through the writings of Major Cartwright and whose elfish appearance—he was small, rotund, and effeminate—belied his belligerent temperament; he soon developed a penchant for haranguing workers at the tavern "sectional houses" in a bombastic style to cries of "Now curly Jack, rattle at 'em, you noes how to do 'em." Parkin recently had settled nearby at Dudley after unsuccessful mercantile and publishing ventures in London, the latest being the editorship of the *Christian Corrector*, and in his new location he quickly earned a reputation as the town demagogue.

These Radicals were important accessions who might have altered the balance of power in the union, had not their influence been offset partially by other new councilmen who were inclined to agree with the Ultra-Tory moderates. The two most important of the new Ultra-Tories were Joseph Biddle, a chemist who was to be an able leader despite his advanced age and his morose disposition, and George de Bosco Attwood, the eldest son of Thomas and an associate in his bank. It was with much reluctance that Bosco was permitted by his father to take an active part in the union, for Thomas feared involving the family in what he believed was a risk of imprisonment; nevertheless, the young man of twenty-three soon became one of the wisest political strategists on the council. The moderates thus maintained their numerical superiority, but the new Radical members joined Russell, Pare, and Edmonds in a campaign of intervention in Birmingham politics that was to give the union greater power locally.

The campaign was never officially authorized by the council. Although one of the stated purposes of the union was "to prevent and redress local public wrongs and oppressions," Attwood and the Ultra-Tories in reality had little interest in reforming the local system of government. Undoubtedly their aristocratic bent disposed them to accept without demur the closed corporation and the jumble of boards overseeing the official business of the town. The Radicals, in contrast, saw nothing good in it and found the union an excellent base from which to conduct operations against it. Because closed towns such as Birmingham regularly elected only the guardians and part of the churchwardens and sidesmen, resistance to policies was possible mainly when one of the governing bodies sought approval from the parish voters for new rates or for authorization to go to Parliament for altered powers. The Radicals now made issues of several such requests. Most of the points of contention related to the Established Church's authority over matters such as the burial ground and the free grammar school, and most of them were only of local interest— although a prolonged fight over church rates had wider significance—but they all generated much heat which was vented in a series of boisterous meetings stretching over a period of eighteen months. In these quarrels the Ultra-Tories on the council generally sided with the corporation and Church party against their fellow unionists even though the Radicals earned popular applause for the union by initiating and directing the hostilities.

In view of these local triumphs there clearly was some basis for the *Journal's* boast that the political "oligarchy" which hitherto had controlled Birmingham politics had been "completely shorn of their strength by the institution of the Political Union." Edmonds asserted that the union had become "an engine of great good, in a local point of view."[7] Yet this was not the purpose for which it was organized, and these local matters entrenched the union's provincialism and diverted its attention and energies from its announced goal of obtaining parliamentary reform as a first step toward other major changes. Once the council had agreed upon Blandford's plan, their task was to organize a concerted national movement for it.

The basic problem in organizing national political agitation was that in most respects it was illegal. Party politics at that time were based principally upon patronage, not "activity." Political meetings were limited to ones called by officials; organizations could not have branches, and their leaders could not correspond with each other; any disorderly conduct by members or by participants in meetings could fasten responsibility upon the organizers for a breach of the public peace; and the laws against sedition were such that forceful speakers automatically incurred the risk of arrest. Attwood from the start resolved to avoid these hazards by adhering to a policy of strict legality. By nature he was a cautious, even timid, man: Parkes was later to declare that physical courage was one of the traits that the banker lacked to be a great agitator.[8] He often expressed his fear of being seized and lodged in a dungeon or otherwise "destroyed like the reformers of old." Thus he determined to follow a course of great discretion.

In accord with this policy, Attwood sought assurances from the attorney general (who refused any comment) and from several eminent lawyers that the *Rules and Regulations* of the union were unobjectionable. Among the lawyers was the head of the Catholic Association, Daniel O'Connell, upon whom Attwood called at Coventry when the Irish agitator was on the way to London.[9] Later the regulations of the union were altered to suspend automatically any member not acting in strict conformity with the law.[10] To lessen the danger of arrest for treasonous language, the council engaged the services of Joseph Parkes, who, having failed to prevent the formation of the union, was now willing to serve it professionally. Parkes hereafter read the slips of the reports of the meetings sent to the newspapers and erased any words which he judged to be seditious.[11] A measure of Attwood's uneasiness on this matter of legality was the invitation to join the union which he extended to Sir Francis Burdett immediately upon a correspondent's remarking that Burdett possessed more experience than any other man in England in avoiding arrest for seditious statements.[12]

There were only two ways for an organization to conduct widespread agitation in Britain without being snared by the home secretary and the attorney general. One method was to encourage the formation of independent but similar societies in other places and to lead them mainly by example. To the degree that communication among them was necessary, it could be effected on a limited basis by public circulars, by advertisements in the press, and by personal visits by deputations, all of which remained legal. Thus Attwood and the council presumably could encourage the formation of numerous other political unions and guide them indirectly in a concerted agitation. The second method was to attract the attention of the London press and to reach a large audience through them and through the numerous local newspapers which copied extensively from them. Hence it theoretically was possible for the leaders of the union by publicity to reach and rouse the middle and lower classes across the country, assuming that distress had made these classes receptive to the directives of the Birmingham union.

The council of the union experimented with both of these methods. From the start Attwood had expected that other towns would hasten to form political unions and that these societies would acknowledge the leadership of the "parent" union at Birmingham. He had no plans to organize the unions elsewhere, but he strongly believed that most communities were ready to follow Birmingham's example. This expectation was reflected in the council's optimistic report to the general meeting in May that the formation of political unions was making rapid progress throughout the country, and in their statement to the meeting in July that organizing activity was going forward in all parts of the kingdom. The fact was, however, that these claims were much exaggerated: the Birmingham society attracted only a fraction of the attention and interest which its founders imagined, and no more than a dozen unions had been formed by the end of July.[13] Only about a score had appeared four months later when Wellington's government fell from power, and perhaps an additional ten to twenty were in existence when the reform bill was introduced in March 1831.[14] Certainly these numbers were not sufficient to frighten many boroughmongers into submission.

A further difficulty for Attwood was the divided character which the political unions promptly exhibited. One of the first of the new unions to appear was the Metropolitan Political Union in London, organized in March 1830 by Henry Hunt and his followers. It catered exclusively to the working classes by advocating a radical program of universal manhood suffrage, annual parliaments, and the ballot, and it quickly emerged as a competing rather than a supporting force to Attwood's society. Many of the unions which were formed subsequently, including about half of those outside of the Midlands, subscribed to Hunt's "Metropolitan principle" and spurned the Birmingham program of moderate reform based upon a union of the middle and lower classes. The council's hope for a multitude of unionist voices faithfully echoing their own thus was frustrated from the very beginning.

Even among the moderate unions the council had little impact. Attwood's decision not to break the law meant that the direct influence of the council was limited to the unions which were located within about thirty miles of Birmingham, these being the ones that could most readily be visited in person by the councilmen.[15] Here the Birmingham leaders were active; but beyond this point they had neither the time nor the finances to intervene personally, even if they had believed there were a chance of control. For these distant unions the council adopted the policy of advertising resolutions in the press and of hoping for some response to them, a practice which offered scant hope of effectual communication. Soon a pattern developed: in all of their public statements the council ignored the independent activities of other unions and pretended that the societies without exception were keenly attuned to the resolutions and directives emanating out of Birmingham. It was a fiction calculated to aid Attwood and his associates in their endeavor by using publicity to gain the leadership of the middle and lower classes nationally, but it was nonetheless a fiction. The small and divided political union movement was not directed from Birmingham in 1830.

The council's alternative strategy called for them to gain publicity in the nation's press sufficient to enlist the middle and lower classes of the kingdom behind the union's demand for parliamentary and other reforms. Attwood believed that the ground for this appeal to the "industrious classes" had been so well prepared by economic distress that all that was needed now was for the union's offer of leadership to become known. It was with great anticipation, therefore, that the Birmingham leaders awaited the reaction of the press and of popular spokesmen elsewhere to the union's initial meetings and pronouncements. It must have been with disappointment equal to this anticipation that they found their efforts to get attention rewarded mostly with indifference and hostility.

The cog of the wheel was the London newspapers, particularly the large dailies. Unfortunately for the council, these newspapers generally were hostile to the new society. Thomas Barnes, editor of *The Times,* called the organizational meeting "nonsense" and declared that the union was nothing more than a device for "forcing upon the nation a fresh dose of the very same poison (namely, one pound notes), from the evacuation of which it is now palpitating . . ."; John Black of the *Morning Chronicle* was more charitable about the possible reformist intentions of the council, but he scoffed at Attwood's predictions of impending economic disaster.[16] These gibes at the union as merely another curiosity spawned by the Birmingham currency party later were echoed in the provincial press. Subsequent meetings and resolutions fared worse, for the London and provincial newspapers gave the union only a fraction of the space it had received in January. Being ignored was worse then being scoffed at. It was obvious that most of the nation's press regarded the widespread meetings of agriculturalists, taking place simultaneously to protest economic distress, as far more significant than the activities of the union—not to mention the greater relative importance which they assigned to the latest sensational developments in the Oddingley murder case at Worcester.

The only fount from which the council could get extensive and favorable publicity was the local *Birmingham Journal,* edited by the High-Tory Jonathan Crowther. The relationship between the union and the *Journal* became symbiotic, for the newspaper's circulation increased greatly as a result of the local publicity it gave the union. The ties between the two proved additionally important as the council failed in an effort to sponsor a new publication in cooperation with the Coventry political union, and as the other Birmingham newspaper, the Tory *Gazette,* grew steadily more hostile to the union.[17] A third newspaper, the *Midland Representative,* appeared the following spring, but it had the young radical James Bronterre O'Brien as editor and it did not alter immediately the special relationship between the *Journal* and the union.

As for reformers outside of Birmingham who might respond to the leadership of the council, most of them took slight notice of the formation of the union and of its early activities, there being nothing in the past record of the principal leaders of the society to command their attention or respect. William Cobbett, the longtime foe of paper currency, virtually alone broke the silence, and he sneered at the idea that men who had "abused the reformers as much as any persons in this kingdom" could now be serious about parliamentary reform.[18] In July, Attwood and Hadley went to London and with much effort persuaded Burdett to come to Birmingham and help establish a national image for the union by presiding over its annual business meeting scheduled for that month. Burdett came as pledged, but the meeting attracted little notice from the press and from other reformers. Finally, the agriculturalists in the country, who already were agitating and who included some Whig reformers actively raising the question of parliamentary reform, totally snubbed the union and its offer of leadership. Indeed, an attempt by the council to intervene in the Warwickshire election in August led only to ridicule of the union by the two candidates, accompanied by whoops of delight from the freeholders gathered at the hustings.[19]

Although the council must have been disappointed with the generally negative response to their early activities, they gave little outward evidence of being disheartened. Attwood declared at the general meeting in May that the effect produced by the formation of the union had "resounded throughout England, and throughout Europe" and had "given the enemy a tremendous blow." When Scholefield during the July meeting conceded that the union had not accomplished much outside of Birmingham, the other speakers quickly contradicted his statement.[20] How, then, is one to reconcile these optimistic declarations with the facts? A partial explanation may be found in the growth of the local power of the union; but much more important was the conspiratorial conception of politics Attwood and his friends held. As the union's threat to the boroughmongers increased, this interpretation suggested, it was to be expected that the forces of evil would reply with stronger efforts to sow division and discord among all groups in society who might unite against them. "The infernal maxim, 'divide and conquer,' is made the fixed policy of the Borough Faction," the council warned in their Report in July. Hence outside suspicion and apathy with respect to the union were not necessarily a sign of weakness in its organization and policies, but rather were an indication that it was beginning to have a serious impact upon the political life of the country. The internal logic of this argument was practically irrefutable, although there was not much else to be said for it.

Thus far the impact of the union outside of Birmingham was hardly perceptible. Yet from this low point of apparent impotency the fortunes of the organization began to rise. The reasons lay mostly beyond the council's range of activity and, indeed, to some extent beyond even their knowledge. Apparently unknown to Attwood and his associates with their provincial interests and heterodox politics, the parties of the opposition were coalescing to oust the Duke of Wellington's Tory government from power. Since the spring a variety of voices, of which the council's was but one, and of which that of the agriculturalists undoubtedly was the most important, had sporadically raised the question of parliamentary reform, not yet to the status of a major issue, it is true, but sufficiently to make it available as a weapon which the Whigs and their allies could bring advantageously against the Duke. A new king, William IV, came to the throne in June and seemed vaguely sympathetic to reform. Abroad there was revolution and at home there was rioting by rural laborers, both of which added a note of urgency to the political scene. The excitement in turn roused to action many radicals who had been relatively quiescent since 1819. In this situation of flux and uncertainty anyone naive enough, or brash enough, to claim the major credit for the changes that took place could easily do so. The council of the Birmingham union qualified because they were both naive and brash. They were soon to claim, and to a remarkable degree they later were to receive, primary credit for all that occurred, winning thereby the national prominence which they so desired and needed.

The news of the French Revolution of 1830 gave the council their first opportunity publicly to associate themselves with great events and to impress the nation. Initial accounts of the French uprising arrived in England during the last days of the election. The council quickly took note of it, and after some indecision over how to react they began to prepare for a massive dinner for 4,000 members of the union to commemorate the Revolution in a truly impressive fashion. In the interval, while preparations were under way, the leaders of the union invaded and took over a small but competing meeting got up by the Whig-Dissenter party to congratulate the French revolutionaries. Next, and more important because it helped justify the council's later claim to national influence, was an address to the king made in maneuvering against these local rivals. In June the council had observed the accession of William IV by advertising a call for addresses to him from throughout the nation apprising the king of the "lamentable state of his *faithful people*";[21] there apparently was no response to the resolution, however, and the council themselves turned to other matters and failed to send any address. Now, in August, they discovered that the Whig-Dissenter party had drafted a loyal address of its own and was quietly circulating it for signatures. The council answered by calling a town meeting to congratulate the king "properly". The address to William passed by this meeting warmly congratulated him on his accession, but it went on to warn him of an alarming state of events arising out of misrepresentation in the House of Commons and it declared that the crown alone could prevent the country from falling into "an irremediable abyss."[22]

The odd mixture of self-assertion and loyal appeal to the throne which appeared in the above meeting manifested itself as well in the dinner of the union to commemorate the July Revolution. The affair was conducted on the grand scale which the council had promised. An estimated 3,500 members purchased tickets for the meal, and several hundred others forced their way past the door-keepers to partake of the bread, meat, beer, and ale provided for the diners. There were flags, performances by the union band and fifty professional singers (whom the audience applauded by striking their plates with the knives and forks), special songs, including the "Union Hymn" and "The Gathering of the Birmingham Union,"[23] and, not least important, numerous toasts. By the middle of the evening the strength of the ale was manifest in almost every face and "friendly congratulations" tended to drown out the official business, despite repeated blasts from the trumpets calling for attention. Several thousand spectators crowded into the room and added to the confusion. Yet by all accounts the proceedings remained peaceful even when the speakers could not be heard beyond the front tables. Attwood was the principal speaker, and following a monetary explanation of the French Revolution, he assured his audience that Englishmen had no need of physical force as long as moral power, "the sword of the spirit," was wielded by the union in dinners such as this.[24]

Only three weeks following this dinner Parliament convened for its new session and the parties of the opposition made their move. Two weeks later the Tory government headed by Wellington fell from power and a coalition headed by Lord Grey and the Whigs came into office. To this point the council had had little to say about party politics, being almost entirely outsiders, and there is no evidence that they suspected the political difficulties which awaited the Duke at the start of the session or knew of his determination to make no concessions to the coalition against him. It apparently was with genuine surprise, therefore, that Attwood and the other union leaders read the Speech from the Throne in which the Tory ministers had the king speak of the general prosperity and happiness of the country. Wellington's simultaneous declaration against the necessity of parliamentary reform undoubtedly also was a surprise. At once the council drew up a petition to the king expressing their "grief and alarm" over these speeches and imploring him to exercise his constitutional power to protect his faithful and loyal people by dismissing from his councils and presence forever the ministers who had so grossly abused his royal confidence. They urged other communities to cooperate with the inhabitants of Birmingham in this appeal to the king and they advertised their petition and resolutions in the *Sun* newspaper in London and in the *Birmingham Journal*.[25]

By the middle of November the Whigs had assumed control of the government and had pledged themselves to sponsor a bill for parliamentary reform. It was a remarkable turn of events. In reflecting back upon these developments, Attwood and his associates on the council concluded that they themselves must have been responsible. The claim was first advanced at a town meeting on December 13, called by Attwood to thank the king for dismissing his old ministers and to pass a resolution of support for the new ones. (The meeting was probably also called to thwart action by Parkes and the Whigs, who had taken preliminary steps for a requisition on the very day that the council acted.) Attwood assured his hearers that the meetings of the union had played an extraordinary role in promoting the great cause of reform in the country. More than that, he said, the union gradually had acquired a truly formidable moral strength which had been used to good effect in the past weeks. First, the council had informed the king of the distress in the country arising from the mismanagement of public affairs, and these words "he [Mr. A.] had the best reason to believe, had been duly digested and considered in his Majesty's Royal mind." Later, when the council had read the speech which his late ministers had put into his majesty's mouth, without hesitation they had asked William to dismiss these ministers. Their petition had been printed in the *Sun* newspaper in London only four days before the crucial vote in Parliament that had defeated the government, and he doubted not, Attwood said, that it must have had an effect upon the minds of the members of the House of Commons. To climax the event, the king had, as the council had requested, appointed new ministers pledged to parliamentary reform. For fifteen years, Attwood concluded, he had foretold famine, bankruptcy, and revolution, and he now rejoiced that he had acquired the power to assist "in arresting the progress of these devastating and destructive contingencies."[26]

There was, of course, no evidence whatever to support the council's version of events. Until midsummer it had been the discontented agriculturalists, not the union, who had commanded the attention of the country. In the final weeks it had been the riots of the rural laborers and the collective agitation of the radicals which had received the major publicity, the October dinner of the union being the only Birmingham event attracting comparable notice. Neither locally nor nationally had Attwood effected a genuine political union of the lower and middle classes. During the past year the union actually had given most of its time to organizational problems and local issues, and, although it unquestionably had contributed generally to the demand for parliamentary reform, a great many other reformers also had contributed. There is no reason to believe that the council's advertised pronouncements had had any effect upon the attitude of the king, to whom the leaders of the union anachronistically directed their attention, or upon the actions of the politicians who actually determined the course of events—or, indeed, that either the king or the politicians even knew of the addresses. In short, the union at this time was neither a powerful engine pulling the rest of England toward reform, as the council claimed, nor was it merely a rear carriage equipped with its own whistle, as its critics later insisted. But clearly in the national politics of 1830 it did little more than carry its own weight.

Yet political fancy can be as important as fact if it is genuinely believed, and the council from their provincial and apocalyptic viewpoint were convinced that the union virtually alone had suddenly altered the course of the nation's history. What other plausible explanation was there for what had happened? The council knew of none. The result was a much greater assertiveness on the part of the union's leaders. At a dinner in January, for example, Attwood reported that the union now had nearly 9,000 members registered on its books, and he proceeded to enlarge their number through the magic lens of "influence."

> Considering the influence which these 9,000 men exercised over the whole population of this town, containing 150,000 souls, and that nearly equal influence which they exercised over the inhabitants of the populous manufacturing towns and districts around them, containing from 2 to 300,000 inhabitants more, the importance of the Union, considered in this light, as influencing a dense population of 400,000 souls, was far too great to be disregarded. The Union had, in fact, condensed the moral power of this great population, and gathered it, as it were, into an electric mass, which was powerful to every good purpose, and utterly impotent to every bad one. Suppose, for instance, their good King should meet with difficulties in his path from the pertinacity of the oligarchy; suppose they should . . . *make fight* upon the occasion: —Why, the very moment the King commanded them, they would produce a national guard that would be like a wall of fire around his throne. (*Cheers.*) It was not too much to say, that if the King required it, they could produce him, in this

district, at his orders within a month, two armies, each of them as numerous and as brave as that which conquered at Waterloo.[27]

As the *Morning Chronicle* commented, Attwood and his Birmingham heroes could have all the merit of their offer without any hazard.[28] Yet the statement, however bombastic, did receive extensive publicity. In the months ahead the union was to play a prominent role in the national agitation for reform largely because its council believed that they had now become national leaders and must act the part.

CHAPTER III

The Union and the Movement for
the Reform Bill
First Phase, January-November 1831

NO MORE THAN ANCIENT CRUSADERS could tolerate Moslem sultans could the English political agitators in theory support ministers who were in power. That at least was the traditional supposition. Yet now that the Whigs had gained office, and according to the council gained it through the union's appeal to the king and the country, it was obvious that Attwood and his associates must support the new government if possible. It was a novel role for most agitators to play, but the leaders of the Birmingham union were uniquely qualified for it. A majority of the members of the council were royalist-minded Ultra-Tories who found respect for constituted authority far more natural than any defiance of it; the campaign they had envisioned from the start was a moral one aimed at an ill-defined oligarchy rather than at flesh-and-blood ministers of the king. They had slight contact with other agitators or with the radical tradition of England. Thus when the movement for parliamentary reform suddenly acquired governmental sponsorship, the council found themselves in the unusual position among agitators of fitting easily into the garb of ministerialists. This fact was to be the key to most of their policies and to much of their influence, real or alleged, during the next eighteen months.

The government's plan of reform, presented by Lord John Russell on March 1, 1831, won the approval of middle-class and moderate reformers throughout the country. Although the plan did not give the franchise to all householders, as the union had demanded, it went further than Blandford had advocated in its destruction of rotten boroughs and its transfer of seats to populous towns and counties. It was, in short, precisely the kind of reform that the Ultra-Tories on the council could endorse. As Attwood reasoned, "a doomed and God-abandoned nation" destined for "the fiery ordeal of terrific miseries" had suddenly been rescued by the introduction of this measure, the most significant event since the signing of the Magna Charta. The reform was the gift of "a patriot King" responding to his people's needs, and the people, headed by the union, must stand by him by defending faithfully his ministers and the bill.[1]

The new political situation seemed likely to lead the union to participate directly in national activity for the first time. Gradually a massive agitation for the reform bill got under way in Britain, one in which old and new organizations met and petitioned for passage of the bill. The middle classes in the towns, led by Whigs and Radicals, roused to agitation, and discontented agriculturalists in the counties, led mostly by Whigs, likewise met in unprecedented numbers. It was probably the first time in British history that reformers had demonstrated in support of the government. Faced with this commotion in its favor, the government relaxed its vigilance against political societies. Thus the Birmingham union seemingly had a unique opportunity during the spring and summer of 1831 to work with other reformers, to establish communication with the government, and perhaps to take the lead in the agitation.

Instead, Attwood and the council remained relatively inactive while the rest of the country met and shouted for the bill. The council advertised several addresses to the country in the press, and they held a routine meeting in Birmingham to thank the king for dissolving Parliament following the defeat of the government in April on a Tory amendment to the bill, but these activities went virtually unnoticed outside of Birmingham. The performance of the union was especially lame for a body that claimed to be guiding the nation in the movement for parliamentary reform.

Attwood and his colleagues believed that the boroughmongers already had been effectively cornered by the alliance of the king and the union. As Hadley put it, "The King, God bless him!

though not actually, is in principle, a member of the Union, and has given his sanction to every measure of Parliamentary Reform brought forward by the Union."[2] All that was necessary now was for the council to support the king's ministers through supplemental addresses and to keep the country quiet while Parliament passed the measure. That the leaders of the union lacked the resources and shunned the contacts to do much more than to issue such addresses was never mentioned and probably was not considered relevant. From the council's conspiratorial interpretation of politics, the danger now seemed to be that of too much activity, not too little. "The inhabitants of Birmingham," Attwood told the union members, "had acquired immense power and influence over the minds of their countrymen, by the combined prudence, justice, moderation, forbearance, and strict legality of all their proceedings." Because millions of their countrymen were prepared instantly to follow Birmingham's leadership, the council had to exercise extreme care lest the excitement got out of hand and justified the employment of suppressive force by the oligarchs.[3]

Even within Birmingham and Warwickshire the pursuit of reform by other groups brought no closer ties between them and the union. The Whig-Dissenter party continued to have nothing to do with the unionists, although the two bodies declaredly now advocated the same cause. The party instead held its own meetings to support the ministers and to petition for passage of the bill. Joseph Parkes, who had a professional association with the union and close contacts with the Whigs, almost alone frequented both tents. Nor did the council find the agriculturalists in the county more interested in cooperation. In April, Attwood and several lieutenants participated in the large Warwickshire reform meeting organized by the Whig gentry, but he displayed the proper deference and made no attempt to interfere with its proceedings, having already learned that the county meetings were a preserve of the gentry and aristocracy not easily poached upon by townsmen.

The refusal by Attwood and the Ultra-Tories to establish greater contact with other agitators caused dissatisfaction among some of the Radicals on the council, who wanted cautious cooperation with the working-class radicals of the country. Most of the radical leaders elsewhere had rejected the reform bill as inadequate and had begun a campaign for a more democratic measure. Chief among them was Henry Hunt, head of the Metropolitan Political Union, whose opposition to the government's measure widened the split between the moderate and the working-class unionist movements. Hunt had visited Birmingham on business in January and had conferred with Attwood after a "continued indisposition" had kept him confined at the Globe Tavern, where the weekly meetings of the council were held. Hunt's companion on the trip, Joseph Mitchell, stated afterward that a basis for collaboration between the two large unions had been laid, but the truth was otherwise, and Attwood was angry about the whole episode.[4] The Radicals on the council urged throughout the spring and summer that the union consider compromises with the radical spokesmen. Attwood, however, stood his ground and rejected any idea of democracy. A deputation sent to the council from the newly formed National Union of the Working Classes in London and the radical unions of Manchester and Blackburn failed to change the banker's mind.[5] Even repeated threats of resignation by some of the Radical councilmen and Russell's actual withdrawal failed to sway him. The fact was that Attwood and his Ultra-Tory associates were not favorable to sweeping reform and there was nothing that could be done at this time to bring them about.

The noisy departure of Russell caused surprisingly little stir in the ranks of the union and failed to prompt further secessions from the council. It was convincing evidence that the cohesiveness of the union was becoming greater than the disruptive tendencies arising out of factionalism within the council. There were major sources of unity now operating to counter schismatic impulses. One of them was the local pride engendered by the myth that the union alone had awakened the nation from its long, torpid repose and had driven Wellington from power by its addresses to the king. Attwood assured the general meeting in July that the union, "like the little Israelitish youth," had gone out against the Goliath of the boroughmongers and had brought it down. The "men of Birmingham" had thereby established their place in history.[6] Another source of unity was the mounting prestige of Attwood among the members of the union, itself partly a product of the myth. This increased standing of the chairman with the members was evidenced by an outpouring of mementos such as portraits of him suitable for display in the members' homes, published songs of tribute, and medals bearing his name and likeness, not to mention the less tangible things such as words of praise and votes of thanks at meetings. Vanity was one of Attwood's weaknesses, and so perhaps he came to believe that the praise was justified, or, as he told a meeting in May, "he would not be so vain as to say that he had entirely undeserved it."[7] Among the Radical councilmen there could be no doubt that his hold was tightening upon the shopkeepers and workers who made up the membership of the union, and they increasingly avoided challenges to his authority, a discretion assisted by the fact that the chairman remained reasonably tolerant of their individual radical ventures.

The union had now become the preponderant factor in Birmingham political life. The Whig-Dissenter and Tory parties could operate only in the shadow of the union, knowing that the council could take over any public meeting by simply ordering the union members to attend the gathering. That the council contemptuously tolerated most of the small meetings got up by their local rivals did not alter their advantage. The source of the council's power lay in the restricted state of politics in the unrepresented towns. Regular party organizations hardly existed. The clusters of local leaders who served as party spokesmen found only limited outlets for active politics: the local parish issues which sometimes provoked heated struggles, and the occasional national movements which aroused emotions sufficient to justify local meetings to petition Parliament or address the king, such as the treatment of Queen Caroline, Catholic emancipation, abolition of slavery, and parliamentary reform. On both of these counts the union now was supreme. The council captured the few elective offices in the parish—churchwarden, sidesmen, and guardians—and they easily controlled all of the parish meetings called to determine public policies. Furthermore, among the populace the political union now was almost wholly identified with the emotional demand for the reform bill. It was the "unionist issue." The council thus had seized the only taps through which political power flowed in the town—they boldly advertised themselves as "the Political Council of the town of Birmingham"—and they were in an advantageous position to continue their control after the reform bill passed.

Yet local supremacy was not the same as national influence. The time for larger things arrived in the fall of 1831. Several major developments were to end the relative quietude of the union and to give it the appearance, if not the substance, of national authority. So decisive were these events in the history of the union that henceforth it would be assured of a place in the radical mythology of Britain.

The first development was an immense meeting held by the union in October to petition the House of Lords for passage of the bill. It was probably the largest political gathering held in Britain to that date, and unquestionably it was the best organized. Yet it was called suddenly and planned hastily, in a belated effort to strengthen support for the government. By the fall of 1831 the ministers had won the election occasioned by the legislative defeat in April and had seen the reform bill through the House of Commons. The fate of the measure now was in the hands of the Lords. Excitement and apprehension mounted throughout the country, generating new meetings everywhere to petition the peers to pass the measure and attracting crowds of a size usually present only at hangings and fairs. Most of the towns around Birmingham had met or were preparing to do so. In contrast, the council thus far had given no indication either of anxiety or of unusual activity. At a large dinner meeting held on September 8 to celebrate William IV's coronation, Attwood and his lieutenants still were congratulating themselves on their victory over the boroughmongers. The union, Attwood said, was truly an electric mass, but there was at the present juncture no cause to call its powers into action.[8] The possibility of new activity was not mentioned during a regular meeting of the council on September 20. Nevertheless, in a special session two nights later the leaders of the union abruptly summoned a great regional meeting for reform to be held at Newhall Hill on October 3.

The decision apparently resulted from an interview which a deputation from the council had with Lord Grey that morning.

This contact with the government officially did not relate to the agitation for the bill—the ministers were careful not to give official sanction to societies agitating for parliamentary reform—but rather it resulted from the impatience of Attwood's faction to do something about the monetary laws. The way was opened for action when the Radicals on the council broke the body's self-imposed ban on discussion of measures other than parliamentary reform. The Ultra-Tory majority on the council gave cursory attention to the Radicals' call for stands against the press laws and against the use of force in Ireland. Then they turned to the question of the currency. They voted to send a memorial to Grey which stressed the necessity of an immediate issuance of paper money, lest the people "be driven to madness" before the reform bill could help matters. They instructed Attwood and four others to deliver the memorial to the prime minister. The request of the deputation for an interview permitted Grey to talk with them about reform without violating his rule against dealing directly with the unions. By now the ministers were deeply concerned about the fate of the bill in the Lords and were increasingly apprehensive over the reaction of the country if the measure failed to pass. Thus Attwood and his associates in their interview with Grey found the prime minister disposed to question them about the mood of their countrymen rather than about the state of the currency. The unionists apparently were surprised and alarmed to learn of the ministers' belief that the bill would not pass. When the deputation returned home that evening they summoned the council and hurriedly issued a call for a public meeting to support the bill.[9]

The decision to meet presented the union with an opportunity to exploit some advantages which the council hitherto had neglected. The agitation for reform in the country was fragmented, with each town and county meeting independently. In most of the large towns the agitation was organized by men who had few official channels of communication with the central government. In the counties the landed Whig leaders generally were in contact with the ministers, but they could not direct matters in the larger towns. What national unity the movement had was provided by the press, as reformers in each area eagerly read about the demonstrations for reform occurring elsewhere. One consequence of the fragmentary nature of the agitation was that the urban meetings, although unprecedented in number, usually were limited to participants from the immediate town. This contrasted with the county meetings, in which the rural reformers gathered from a large area, although they generally comprised only freeholders. Even more serious for the agitators, the friction within the towns between working-class radicals and moderate reformers meant that the reformers, fearful of radical excesses, were inhibited in their willingness to risk large demonstrations. Many middle-class leaders preferred meetings which were kept small and secure; in a few places, such as Liverpool, they chose not to agitate at all. On each of the above counts the Birmingham union had an advantage. It had direct contact with fifteen to twenty other unions in surrounding towns and could enlist them in a *regional*, urban meeting for reform. The other unions could help provide both numbers and spectacle. Furthermore, the relative conservatism of the Birmingham workers, plus the influence of the union locally, made a massive gathering seem less dangerous than was the case in other places. Thus it was that the council, despite some trepidation, decided to risk as large a meeting as all the means of generating excitement could muster.

The day of the meeting was ushered in by the ringing of church bells, and by ten o'clock the inhabitants, summoned by bell ringers in the streets, were on the move toward Newhall Hill, the large clearing of land in the northwest part of town where the event was to take place. Later in the morning Attwood and the council, carrying white wands of office and accompanied by a uniformed band and numerous banners, led a grand procession of union members to the hill site. While the council made their way with difficulty through the crowd to the platform, consisting of a semicircle of wagons placed at the foot of the slope, the men carrying the banners moved up and stationed themselves along the top of the ridge, helping to give the whole scene a festive appearance. Neighboring unions arrived in processions with their own bands and flags, and they were greeted with loud cheers by the people already assembled. The estimates of the crowd varied greatly; the lowest of course was supplied by the Tories, who declared that at no time could the crowd have exceeded 50,000 people, and the median came from other observers and from the persons responsible for the official *Proceedings* and the petitions, all of whom calculated attendance at 100,000. During the course of the meeting, nevertheless, one of the speakers proudly referred to the "150,000 men" before him, and the council afterward adopted this more impressive number as their own estimate.[10] Most outsiders accepted the figure. The credibility of the estimate undoubtedly was furthered by Lord Wharncliffe's citation of it in denouncing the union's "intimidation" of Parliament, and by its inclusion in much-publicized replies written by Russell and Lord Althorp to resolutions of thanks voted them by the meeting.[11]

It should be noted that the attendance was not restricted to *men* or to *active* participants. The crowd included "tens of thousands of beautiful women" by Attwood's own statement (deleted in a second version of the *Proceedings*) and countless children also were present. Bosco wrote his mother after the meeting that the women and children almost equaled the men in number, and a reporter made the same observation.[12] Furthermore, beyond the front third of the large slope the crowd could hear little because of the distance from the speakers and because of the constant movement of people. Most of the persons occupying this rear ground were there as spectators rather than as participants, and so they exhibited, as one reporter observed, "every appearance of holiday-making." Presumably the vendors of food and drink, so much in evidence at subsequent meetings, were active at this initial one too. And yet the actual presence on the field of these observers who previously had lined the streets to watch the processions was highly advantageous, for in outside reports the words "people present" got translated into "men participating." It was a major accomplishment for the council to have attracted so large a gathering to one spot for a political purpose, including in its muster unions from parts of three counties, regardless of the circumstances which prevailed during the meeting itself.

The speeches of the leaders were appropriate to the occasion. Naturally there were frequent allusions to the power of the union, and Attwood in particular exhibited his usual odd mixture of aggressiveness and caution. The Birmingham union, he boasted, "had united two millions of men peaceably and legally in one grand and determined association to recover the liberty, the happiness, and the prosperity of the country, and he should like to know what power there was in England that could resist a power like this?" But he repeated his conviction that the union's influence had spread only because it had kept wholly within the law. To demonstrate their loyalty and thankfulness to the king, he had the whole assembly take off their hats, look reverently toward heaven, and cry out, "God bless the King." One of the Radicals, speaking afterward, apparently represented the more belligerent members when he argued a right of resistance to "tyrants" and asked, to the accompaniment of loud cheers, if the Lords dared refuse to pass the bill. Later Edmonds talked of a nonpayment of taxes if all else failed, a threat then being advanced by many radicals in the country. Amid such declarations the meeting petitioned the peers to approve the measure, but—a precaution—it also passed a memorial to Grey requesting that he remain in office should the Lords fail in their duty.[13]

By working all night, Parkes and the staff of the *Birmingham Journal* produced a long report of the proceedings and sent it off to the *Morning Chronicle* and *The Times*;[14] both newspapers printed three columns of it on the 5th. The provincial press carried much shorter reports several days later. The petition from the meeting was presented by Lord Brougham to the House of Lords on the evening of October 4. Although it was only one of hundreds sent to the House requesting passage of the bill, the size of the meeting and the reported statements of some of the speakers provoked words of censure by several of the Tory peers the following night. Brougham and Grey answered that it was a petition couched in constitutional language from a large body of persons, and that the intemperate words of one or two speakers did not alter the fact that the meeting reflected the nation's feeling about reform.[15]

Two days later the Lords rejected the bill. The news of the division on the measure reached throughout most of England before the next morning. The reactions everywhere were surprise, dismay, and anger. At Birmingham, an express from the London *Sun* arrived at five in the afternoon; a crowd had gathered around the newspaper offices to await the news, and a wild scramble for the papers ensued. The *Midland Representative* immediately issued a special edition carrying the report, and groups of reformers commandeered the church bells to inform the populace beyond the reach of the press. The bells were muffled, and "each Bell," Attwood wrote his wife afterward, "complained to the others in solemn melancholy all night long. It was the dirge of the Oligarchs re-echoing in the heart of England." Attwood added, "Everything is perfectly peaceful & will be so. Do not you have any kind of uneasiness, for you may depend upon my prudence & discretion. The firmness of the king, of his ministers, & of the House of Commons is undoubted."[16] And in fact there were very few incidents of disorder in Birmingham, despite the daily presence of excited groups on the streets and in the taverns. On the 10th a riot narrowly was averted when antireformers removed from St. Philip's one of the black flags which a councilman as churchwarden had ordered flown from that and other parish churches; constables restored peace by restoring the flag. That evening roving bands broke the windows of several of the houses in St. Mary's Square, including those of two of the councilmen. But thereafter the town remained quiet.[17]

In this matter of peacekeeping the council rendered a special service to the government. In temperament and philosophy Attwood and his associates were far too removed from political reality to be really effective national agitators. They merely had the good fortune during these months to be part of an overpowering national movement for reform; even their Newhall Hill meeting was only one voice, however loud, in a great chorus of demands for the passage of the bill. But in urging calm at this moment of reversal, on the ground that the bill eventually must pass, the council could speak with greater conviction than could most reformers. From the council's standpoint, the boroughmongers remained defeated so long as the king who had responded to their addresses remained on the throne and so long as his choice of reforming ministers remained in office. The danger consistently had been that the agitation would get out of hand and give the desperate boroughmongers a chance to plunge the country into anarchy; Attwood's frequently repeated fear of upheavals was a very real one for him. Thus, while other reform leaders in the country similarly preached confidence in the government and labored to keep the people quiet, the council, backed by the prestige of their recent meeting, unquestionably spoke with a voice more persuasive than the rest.

Within an hour after word of the adverse vote of the Lords reached Birmingham, Attwood and several others on the council got together and drew up the following address:

> Friends and Fellow Countrymen! The Bill of Reform is rejected by the House of Lords! Patience! Patience!! Patience!!! Our beloved King is firm—his patriot ministers are firm—the House of Commons is firm—the whole nation is firm. What then have the people to fear? Nothing! — unless their own violence should rashly lead to anarchy, and place difficulties in the way of the King and of his Ministers. Therefore there must be no violence. The people are too strong to require violence. By peace—by law—by order—every one must rally round the throne of the King. The small majority of the Lords will soon come to a sense of the duty which they owe to their Country and to the King—or some other legal means will be devised of carrying the Bill of Reform into a law without delay. Fellow countrymen—be patient—be peaceful—be strictly obedient to the laws, and every thing is yet safe. God bless the King!

They quickly had the address posted in all sections of town, and the following day they forwarded several thousand copies by the coaches to all parts of the kingdom,[18] with most of them presumably going to newspaper offices and political unions for further circulation. The document appeared in the London newspapers on the 10th, only three days after the vote by the Lords and in time to have some possible influence upon other reformers.

The council also took steps to make public locally the replies of Russell, Althorp, and a Warwickshire M.P. to the resolutions of thanks voted them by the meeting on October 3. All three letters were written just after the vote by the Lords, and all urged restraint. Russell wrote, "It is impossible that the whisper of a faction should prevail against the voice of a nation"—a phrase that provoked a storm of criticism in both Parliament and Court—and Althorp declared that the negative vote of the peers could do no more than delay the passage of reform.[19] Althorp went on to criticize the words used by Edmonds at the meeting; Attwood replied that they were merely hypothetical; and Althorp again vouched for the safety of reform so long as the country remained peaceful. Although the letters were to Attwood as chairman of a meeting rather than as chairman of the union, Attwood used them effectively at the council meeting on the 11th in urging calm upon the two thousand excited members who crowded the chamber, stairways, and the street outside. He had just heard from the government, and "every thing seemed to be going on right," Attwood told them; they must continue to place confidence in the council.[20] The impression that the chairman was in close, constant communication with the government must have been greatly reassuring to the members.

The degree of influence which the council's address to the nation had outside of the Midlands is, of course, uncertain. Local reform leaders everywhere sought to maintain order, and the key factors which they stressed in their speeches were the passage by the Commons on the 10th of Lord Ebrington's motion of unabated confidence in the ministers, and Lord Althorp's response that the government would remain in office and introduce a new reform bill. But references were also made, especially in the press, to the beneficial effect that the council's appeal had produced. A safe conclusion is that the council for the first time exercised some direct, if modest, influence upon the country as a whole.

The council issued further documents, supplementing the above address, during the following weeks. On October 13, the leaders of the union held a special session to adopt a strongly worded petition to the House of Commons to act upon a new bill without delay. Their action seems to have resulted from the prompting of Joseph Parkes, who himself swayed by the excitable Francis Place, had persuaded them that the ministers might compromise with the antireformers.[21] A week later the council addressed the country and called for the formation of political unions in every town and village. This address revealed that the council had returned fully to a position of trusting the government: "Our road is clear. Our mind is made up. We will stand by Lord Grey."[22]

In their next major action during these weeks of tension, the council overstepped themselves and yet, in backing down, attracted major publicity and considerably enhanced their national image. It was a long-standing radical tenet that the strength of agitators was proportional to the challenge which they could mount against the government. In the present novel situation in which moderates demonstrated for a ministerial measure, it was at least necessary for agitators occasionally to evidence some independence of the government, to prove that they were crusaders who bore arms as well as banners. The council now won some recognition in this respect. The incident grew out of the perplexity and fear which gripped the country in the aftermath of the defeat of the bill. Radicalism seemed everywhere on the increase, with working-class radicals boldly intruding into meetings called by moderates, and with middle-class men such as Place preaching distrust of the government. There were widespread rumors of arming; and seemingly giving substance to the rumors, there were riots at Derby, Nottingham, and Bristol. Several of the London newspapers took alarm and began to urge greater organization by reformers to maintain order and secure passage of the bill: one development which in their opinion would fulfill this need was the organization of additional political unions, something already taking place spontaneously throughout the country. Another step was the formation of a national guard of armed volunteers to preserve order and protect property.[23]

The council of the Birmingham union was the one body most likely to respond to the warnings of danger. Attwood long had feared convulsions in the country, and he now cautioned the council that the enemy had spies abroad who were encouraging riot and tumult. The banker and his Ultra-Tory associates were strongly inclined to the protection of property, and those persons who corresponded and talked with the Birmingham leaders at this time sensed that their anxiety was deep-seated. Althorp wrote his father that "the leaders of the political unions are . . . frightened, as they find they have set a machine in motion which they cannot control"; and Parkes wrote of Attwood's lack of courage and declared, "I know every leader of the Union. I know they do not mean to lead the people, and will not."[24] The Bristol riot especially was upsetting to Attwood, for he had held that no disturbances would take place in towns that possessed active political unions.[25] At the first three sessions of the council in November, the chairman and his associates accordingly reconsidered the situation within Birmingham and discussed the propriety of restructuring the union along military lines "to render the physical powers of the Union available for the preservation of life and property." A committee drafted a plan to subdivide the organization into branches and units, with officers at each level (distinguished by appropriate badges and staffs) to whom the members would be pledged to obey. The members would not be armed, Attwood emphasized, but they would be available promptly to suppress riots, presumably by the sheer weight of their numbers.[26]

The plan immediately attracted the attention of the press throughout the nation and aroused the concern of the government. It obviously was a portentous departure in British politics for any self-appointed body to undertake to keep the peace, and if the union succeeded in its purpose the way presumably would be opened for any group professing uneasiness about public tranquillity to assume deterrent powers. Making the matter a cause for greater speculation was that the council had often boasted of their willingness to fight for the king. Those persons close to the council knew that such talk was pure braggadocio, but those farther away did not. The council's discussion of "policing," therefore, was widely reported as "arming," despite Attwood's emphatic denials that such was contemplated. Other bodies in any case were likely to consider arms as essential to their task of peace-keeping. The Birmingham union seemingly was the test whether this new direction in agitation was to be taken.

The government had no choice but to prevent it. The whole affair undoubtedly headed the list of "difficulties & annoyances" caused by the friends of reform which Grey declared to "surpass all imagination."[27] For one thing, numerous other unions were being formed, and the ministers did not know what connection, if any, the new societies had with Birmingham. Considering the degree of excitement still prevailing in the country, it seemed foolish to antagonize publicly an organization that recently had helped to maintain order. Althorp sought a way out of the dilemma by asking Parkes, one of the few Radicals with whom he had been communicating regarding the provisions of the new bill, privately to "try to influence Mr. Attwood not to proceed in the organization of the Political Union." Parkes then went to Attwood and Scholefield and told them that the proposed plan was illegal; as usual he found the banker highly sensitive to any such possibility.[28] The council held their weekly session on the 22nd. Parkes attended it and explained the law to the other leaders of the union, following which they reluctantly voted to abandon the plan. In the meantime the government, fearful that other unions would disregard the lead of Birmingham, drew up a proclamation against hierarchically organized associations and posted it on the very evening that the council met. The outcome was that the union's leaders claimed much credit for voluntarily keeping within the law and the government claimed credit for its firmness in handling the union—although many observers suspected collusion.[29] The affair was a considerable gain for the council in that they achieved for a second time some of the national prominence which they coveted. Ironically, once again they did so more through an effort to restrain radical activity than by a promotion of further agitation.

By the time the government issued its proclamation the alarm in the country finally had begun to subside. Many radical leaders worked hard at keeping the excitement going, but with diminishing results. *The Times* and the *Morning Chronicle* perhaps signaled the turn of things when they backed off from their call for a national guard.[30] The council soon exhibited a similar change of mood. They no longer spoke of the country as ignited gunpowder, and they grew reluctant to adopt further addresses to the king and Parliament lest their action be deemed "intrusive." On December 12 the ministers presented a third reform bill to the House of Commons, and the measure proved to be fully as strong as the one that the Lords had rejected. The council at their session the next day reviewed the measure and avowed themselves completely satisfied. The boroughmongers had been successfully routed, they decided, and now the union had only to resume its policy of trusting the king and his chosen ministers to finish off the enemy, aided by the moral power of the union.[31]

CHAPTER IV

The Union and the Movement
for the Reform Bill

Second Phase, December 1831–June 1832

SHIFTS OF POWER in the midst of complex campaigns are deceptive and therefore are difficult to assess, and so it was that the events of October and November advanced the fortunes of the union less dramatically than the council and many others believed. An exaggerated estimate of the power now wielded by the council resulted in part from the enthusiastic response of the members to their leadership: the rank and file of the union had followed orders to remain calm and they had shown such an interest in the opinions of their leaders that they had crowded the council's chamber at the Globe beyond sufferance, forcing the speakers to stand on the table to be seen and heard, and frequently overflowing into the corridor and down the stairway into the street outside. The council soon appointed a committee to seek new quarters; in March, the "parliamentary chamber" and the offices of the union were both removed to a renovated building located at the upper end of Great Charles Street. The new chamber was long and commodious, with the council's table and adjacent seats for visitors at one end and, separated by a low but strong partition, a gallery for five hundred spectators in the remainder of the room. The banners of the union decorated the walls and an elegant gas lamp hung above the table. The quarters amply befitted men whom, Muntz declared, were looked to with intense interest by the whole world.

The council indeed had achieved considerable prominence outside of Birmingham. The Newhall Hill meeting, the calls for order and for patience, and the talk of reorganizing the union unquestionably had caught the attention of the nation. Although a multitude of other groups had been equally active and concerned, none seemed to possess the council's unusual combination of boastfulness, based upon a large and devoted following, coupled with a policy of extreme caution. The national reputation of the council was furthered also by the propaganda war which followed the rejection of the bill. Many antireformers were looking for some identifiable culprits behind the excitement, and many reformers were prepared to applaud the deeds of anybody so selected. Hence when the Tory *Standard* led the way in charging that the leaders of the Birmingham union were responsible for the recent disorders, and even that they had dispatched thousands of armed men secretly into Bristol and London,[1] the accusations, unwarranted as they were, apparently convinced many reformers that the union had the ability to do what was said. There were rumors as well that the council were in constant, secret communication with the ministers. Tories and radicals alike spread these stories concerning the union's relationship with the government. It was useless for the council to deny the rumors, since most of the opponents of the bill, and many of its friends, preferred to believe that they were true.

Another factor which enhanced the standing of the Birmingham leaders was the rapid spread of political unions during this period. The fear of disorders and the uncertainty over what political action to take prompted men all over the country to establish unions. The most prominent was the National Political Union in London, organized by Place and his circle as a counter to the Rotunda radicals; and the most active was the National Union of the Working Classes, which was sponsored by these Rotunda radicals and which illegally established twelve branches in the metropolis and thirty in the provinces.[2] Many of the new societies, both radical and moderate, apparently modeled their organization after that of the Birmingham union: the council reported during the crisis that the union had received requests from fifty places for copies of its *Rules and Regulations*.[3] By November there were approximately one hundred unions in the country, varying greatly in their political complexion and ranging in size from a few dozen men in village organizations—the Stratford-on-Avon union had 144 members—to the thousands in the Birmingham union. To observers in all parties it must have appeared, as Lord Duncannon wrote Grey, that the societies had been formed "in every county & almost every parish in England."[4] What specific connection the new unions had with the council at Birmingham was generally unknown to these observers, but in the absence of evidence to the contrary it was widely assumed that they took orders from the "parent society."

Actually, most of these assumptions regarding the national power of the council were without foundation. Even though the chieftains of the union had achieved the publicity breakthrough which they earlier had desired, real leadership did not follow from greater prominence. The factional divisions and local orientation of the reformers in the country precluded it. By now there were four major categories of parliamentary reformers active in the agitation: Whigs, Radicals, some Ultra-Tories (a majority of this faction eventually opposed the bill as too destructive of traditional interests), and radicals, many of whom wanted a bill stronger than the ministerial one. There was little concert among the supporters of the bill, either on a national or on a local basis. Through the press they were aware of each other, yet they looked separately to the government to get the bill through Parliament. Thus the reformers in effect formed separate crusading armies following separate routes, and though Attwood's Birmingham Political Union undeniably had attracted the attention of the others, they did not join forces with him on that account.

Indeed, Attwood did not attempt to unite the varied contingents of reformers. The only band outside of Birmingham with whom he would have readily associated were the ministerialists, but they were not prepared to consort with unionists. Grey himself avoided any close contact with the potentially militant groups who supported the reform bill without adopting Whiggish philosophy. There is no trace of communication between the government and the Birmingham union following Russell's and Althorp's letters to Attwood in October. Nor were there further messages delivered by Parkes following the reorganization episode in November.[5] The ministers remained warily mindful of the union, of course, and they sought Parkes's advice partly because he was in a position to give "the best information as to the feelings of the Unionist Reformers."[6] But they were mindful also of most other reformers in the country and, apart from their concern to prevent Attwood's precipitating a movement for a national guard, they apparently did not regard the Birmingham union as a factor of overriding importance. In their letters to each other it was the country and the unions as a whole that were the subjects generally mentioned, not Attwood and the council individually. Probably their private opinion of Attwood was accurately expressed by Lady Lyttelton, sister of Althorp, who recorded that he "is so entirely absorbed by the currency question that he is reckoned rather cracked about it, otherwise a most amiable good man."[7]

The local ministerialists of Birmingham and Warwickshire likewise were not prepared to cooperate with the unionists. The "respectable classes" of the city seem generally to have approved of the way in which the council had helped to keep the peace during the recent crisis, and some of them said so, but few if any of them joined the union because of it. The orthodox Whig-Dissenter politicians continued to regard Attwood and his friends as strange men with whom serious cooperation in politics was unthinkable. Nor did the Whig agriculturalists of the county draw any closer to them; at a Warwickshire meeting held to protest the vote of the Lords, the county's aristocracy and gentry entrusted to Attwood the movement of a minor resolution, but they themselves completely dominated the proceedings. The council, for their part, appeared now to concede to these landed men the question of rural leadership, explaining "that it was better to leave the freeholders of the county to their own independent expression of public opinion."[8]

Ties between the council and radicals of all stripes continued to be almost nonexistent. Attwood and his faction still maintained their antagonism toward the Huntite radicals of both the London and the Lancashire branches. At least twice during this period they condemned Hunt roundly for his "highly reprehensible" conduct in support of radical reform.[9] The working-class radicals, in turn, were suspicious because of the council's rumored collusion with the government, and many of them began to view the Birmingham union as a tool of the ministers. Cobbett asserted that such was the case unquestionably, and Richard Carlile, holding to his previous verdict that Attwood was either a "rogue or a fool," now thundered, "Damnation to your patience."[10] As for the moderate Radical leaders in the country, there is no evidence at all of serious consultation with Attwood and his associates after November. Even Place's Westminster circle relied upon Parkes, who corresponded from Birmingham with various Benthamites in London, for what intimations they had of the council's thinking.

The relationship of the council with the new political unions also reflected the doctrinal and regional differences among reformers. Cooperation with the radical unions still was contingent upon the union's adoption of radical reform, something Attwood was not prepared to do. The more moderate unions were formed mostly as a safeguard against unknown dangers, not to pursue any definite line of action. The council's unionist activities therefore followed the pattern existing before October, that is, a close association with those within a twenty-five to thirty mile radius of Birmingham, but little with the ones farther away. The chief councilmen spoke frequently at meetings of the neighboring unions, both new[11] and old, and occasionally some of the leaders of these societies attended sessions of the council, where they were introduced simply as "friends of reform." All of these neighboring unions were free to act independently, and did so on various issues, but they clearly regarded themselves as satellites of the Birmingham organization. Farther away, in contrast, there continued to be almost no contact between the council and other unions. For example, the new societies at Leicester, Derby, Nottingham, and Gloucester, which lay just beyond easy reach, seem to have acted without reference to Birmingham after they were founded.[12] The smaller unions in most areas of the country gravitated toward control by the largest one in each region, and thus the Leeds, Manchester, Bristol, and London unions attracted subordinate bodies just as Birmingham did. The council at Birmingham presumably possessed the addresses of many of these other unions, yet they seem never to have broken the law by trying to correspond with them. A lawful alternative, in the form of a monthly *Political Union Register* which would publish dispatches and thereby open up a medium of communication, was started in March 1832, but it failed after only two issues.[13]

The divisions among the reformers continued to be reflected within the Birmingham union itself. Attwood's Ultra-Tory followers maintained their majority on the council, for as resignations occurred—there was a constant turnover of membership on the body—replacements were found. The Ultra-Tories were drawn almost entirely from the ranks of merchants and small manufacturers, and, judging from the frequency with which their names appeared on the bankruptcy lists, most were marginal operators. Nobody of real ability was added, although John Giles, a young manufacturer of engines, William Trow, a ropemaker, and William Jennings, a brassfounder, were to take a modest part in the council's proceedings. The Radicals on the council also included some small businessmen, but a large portion of this group were professional men. (Only one worker, an operative named James Bibb, sat on the council before the advent of Chartism, and he soon resigned.) Most of the new Radical councilmen were as inactive in unionist business as were a majority of the Ultra-Tories, although a few participated effectively, notably Matthew P. Haynes, a young Catholic teacher who had moved recently from Walsall, and two clergymen, the Rev. Thomas Michael McDonnell and Dr. Arthur S. Wade. McDonnell was a tall, thin, middle-aged, bespectacled Catholic priest with a flowery eloquence and an ardent admiration for O'Connell.[14] Dr. Wade, the nonresident vicar of St. Nicholas, Warwick, leaned toward radicalism and was the only extremist on the council. Parkes described the eccentric vicar as a "living Huntite" and "a man of no private character." Certainly, Wade's vituperative language won him an extensive reputation as a political speaker, and his self-indulgent appearance—he was extremely fat, and his pumpkin-round head and large nose and eyes were accentuated by receding hair, long and wiry sideburns, and a small chin—prompted Parkes to add to the above judgment, "Tell [Francis] Place God writes a legible hand writing on every man's face, and to look at Dr. Wade's."[15]

Under the leadership of the newcomers, the Radicals on the council renewed their efforts to enlist the workers and shopkeepers of the union behind a campaign against taxes on knowledge, factory conditions, the treatment of Ireland, and other Radical causes. Their efforts were given additional impetus by the support of these issues furnished by O'Brien and the *Midland Representative*, founded in the spring. The Ultra-Tories opposed these moves on the ground that petitions on subjects other than parliamentary reform were untimely and would embarrass the government; the Radicals suspected that the known indifference of their associates to nonmonetary questions was the real motive. On one occasion Wade and Haynes paid an unauthorized visit to the Metropolitan Political Union, apparently in an attempt to draw the two unions closer.[16] Shortly thereafter Muntz suddenly resigned after declaring that he would not act further with a body of men who suffered a minority that consistently opposed the majority.[17] Muntz was replaced by William Boultbee, a retired Hertfordshire squire who lived at Edgbaston. Boultbee, a large man with a broad face, sharp nose, and bushy white hair, held views not greatly different from those of Muntz, but unlike Muntz he was a man of retiring habits and limited talents. Undoubtedly, the Ultra-Tory leadership of the council was weakened by Muntz's departure.

Although the Radicals caused considerable turmoil within the council, they did not succeed in winning the workers and shopkeepers away from Attwood's leadership. The professed devotion of the members to the chairman seemed never to waver; in February, a deputation presented the "venerated Founder" with a grand address signed by 25,000 persons (reported also as "men" or "members," although even with the accessions during the recent weeks there probably were no more than 15,000 men in the union). The address declared that Attwood's fame would outlast the pyramids of Egypt, and the signers promised, "We will emulate our revered Founder of Political Unions, and walk in his light; we are ready with purse, heart, hand, and head, to aid him and you in the common cause."[18] The alliance between the Radicals and the Ultra-Tories in Birmingham clearly would continue only on Attwood's terms, and the Radicals could do little but accept this fact.

As usual in these matters, Attwood had an explanation for the failure of the council to unite the various bands of reformers in the country. Nothing that had happened in October and November was sufficient to cause him to change his approach to politics, and so it was easily held that the boroughmongers in the midst of death throes had tried to foment violence and discord after the defeat of the bill, and that the council had thwarted them by pursuing a policy of strict legality. Hence it continued to be the moral force exercised by the council that really mattered, not organizational ties. Attwood occasionally expressed concern over the lack of cooperation among reformers, but he gave no indication that it was any of his business to lead them other than by example.

During these months the council did nothing to prepare for the approaching hour when the Lords again would decide the fate of the reform bill. Although pressure came from within the union for further agitation, Attwood and a majority of the council resisted it. In March, some of the members sent an address to their leaders suggesting a public meeting to petition the Lords to pass the bill. Attwood replied that "he thought the time had arrived when they should determine never again to petition that House on the subject of Reform."[19] Another memorial early in the next month met with the same response. The council's attitude subsequently alternated between a feeling of confidence that the boroughmongers already were defeated, and therefore the bill, in Attwood's words, was "perfectly safe," and the opposite extreme of deep anxiety going beyond even that expressed by other agitators. At a session of the unionist leaders on April 10, for example, Attwood declared that they were in "a most awful situation." What they might do remained unclear, however, since Attwood talked one moment of a "grand simultaneous movement" of the country and in the next he declared that great restraint must be exercised in Birmingham in order to set a peaceable example for the nation.[20]

Three days after this meeting the peers passed the second reading of the bill by a majority of nine. The House then adjourned for three weeks' Easter recess, during which negotiations continued between the government and the "waverers" among the antireformist peers who had voted for the second reading. The Tories requested modifications of the measure in committee and Grey maintained that nothing substantial could be conceded. Most of the moderate reformers in the country meanwhile expressed relief over the victory of April 13 and continued uneasily to rely upon the ministers. In contrast, many of the radicals suspected that a compromise by the government was imminent, and they called for meetings to block it. A few places responded, but they were the exceptions; the prevailing attitude was to wait and see. Certainly this appears to have been the policy of the council, whose principal item of business at their weekly session on April 17 was the selection of their candidate for churchwarden; no other topic was mentioned in the reports of their deliberations.

Yet the following week the council suddenly appointed a committee to consider holding a large public meeting, and three days later they summoned the inhabitants of the region to meet on May 7 at Newhall Hill. What had happened to change their minds? Nothing on the part of the government or Parliament adequately explains the decision. Public politics at the moment was in abeyance, as the ministers and the compromising Tories alike worked on the king, with Grey appealing to William for a promise to create peers and with the Tories offering, amid increasing signs of royal favor, a compromise bill. Neither side, of course, knew what the outcome would be. What appears to have stirred the council was not a threat to the bill as such, but rather a threat to their image as undisputed popular leaders.

The attack on them was originated by one of the radicals. On April 21 William Cobbett received a letter from an unidentified patron of a London bookshop who claimed that Parkes had told both the proprietor and himself that reformers would have to accept compromises by the government. Cobbett already was convinced that a sellout of the bill was imminent and that the unions were being primed to acquiesce in it. That Parkes was known to be in contact with both the Birmingham union and the ministers now seemingly confirmed all of his suspicions. Highly excited, he drafted a circular "To the People of Birmingham and to the Reformers in all the Great Towns," printing the letter and warning them to "Be on the alert!" because "some at least of *the Political Unions* [meaning the Birmingham one] would not, upon this occasion, act as they ought to do."[21] He demanded a prompt answer from Parkes, and when he did not get it he sent copies of the circular to the newspapers. The first impulse of the council upon receiving the circular was to address Grey in polite but firm terms and thus to demonstrate the union's true position. Some reflection, however, showed that this might be construed as a statement of distrust in the prime minister, and so the council decided instead to summon another great Newhall Hill assembly to petition the Lords to pass the bill unchanged.[22]

Once resolved upon, it was imperative that the May 7 meeting equal or surpass in spectacle the meeting of October 3. Both the reputation of the council and the cause of reform seemed to be at stake. At once the council set to work enlisting the forty or so neighboring political unions with whom they had contact. A major concern for the council was their fear that disorders might mar the meeting and expose them to the "tentacles of the law." Much of the confidence which Attwood had possessed the previous October had disappeared in the wake of the November riots. Enemies might well be sent among the Birmingham masses to incite violence and illegality, he warned. A measure of his anxiety was that at the end of the all-night session in which the council decided to call the assembly he, according to one of the participants, "fell down upon his knees, and prayed fervently to God, that, 'if the meeting they were about to call, was not calculated to benefit their country, he would intercept his divine power to prevent it.' "[23] Clearly the leaders of the union were acting under pressure and with much reservation about the advisability of holding the meeting they were summoning.

But all went well on the appointed day. The meeting was fully as spectacular and peaceful as the previous one. Excellent weather brought out the populace early, and by ten o'clock crowds had begun to gather on the slope of Newhall Hill and outside the union offices. Several councilmen, designated as marshals, rode to the outskirts of town and escorted the visiting unions to the space reserved for them. Shortly before noon Attwood and the rest of the council led a large procession of members from Great Charles Street to Newhall Hill. As they took their places on the platform at the foot of the hill the leaders could see stretched before them a vast host of followers and spectators, many with banners and flags. Even the tops of the houses adjoining the field were occupied by onlookers.

The speeches and business followed closely the format of the October meeting. Attwood evoked immense cheering when he declared that he would rather die than see the great bill of reform rejected or mutilated, and he was answered by shouts of "All, All!" when he asked his hearers, "Had not you all rather die than live the slaves of Boroughmongers?" Yet he affirmed once more that the power of the union depended upon a strict and dutiful obedience to the law, and he urged his audience never to suffer any circumstance whatever to seduce them into illegal or violent proceedings. Edmonds probably made the most radical speech of the day, declaring that the Lords surely possessed too much sense to reject the bill another time, but if they did refuse it, "their Lordships had better take lessons of the dancing-masters, to qualify themselves for situations on the continent, and their ladies should become proficient at the wash tub." The only indication of what the council proposed to do if the Lords ignored such warnings was the resolution passed by the meeting vowing that in the event of defeat they would never cease to use every legal exertion to obtain a bill surpassing this one.[24]

The publicity given the meeting by the London newspapers was immediate and extensive. The *Morning Chronicle* received the *Birmingham Journal's* report at three o'clock on the morning following the meeting and printed five columns of it in that day's edition. *The Times* sent two reporters of its own to Birmingham and printed a full page of their report on the 9th. The estimates of attendance this time were fairly uniform, for the council had taken steps to prevent discrepancies such as had occurred in October. They provided reporters with "an authentic statement" of the number that came into Birmingham from the surrounding districts (150,000 persons) and added the population of Birmingham and environs (140,000) to the figure, giving the official estimate that, potentially, almost 300,000 persons were available for the meeting. Since according to previous statements the field could accommodate only 150,000 participants and spectators, the official calculation was that "at least 200,000 persons" were present on the hill and congregated in adjoining streets. Attwood used this figure in his speech—not half of the people, he admitted, could come within the hearing of his voice—and most outsiders accepted it. Also, the presence of many thousands of straw bonnets and infants' heads in the crowd as before did not prevent the assembly from becoming "brave and determined men" in subsequent statements, and this despite protests from the antireformist *Standard* that the 1831 census gave only 186,000 adult males in all of Warwickshire and Staffordshire combined.[25]

Whatever the true figure for attendance—and undoubtedly Russell's estimate of 100,000 persons "within sight of each other" was more realistic than the claim issued by the council—the meeting was a success both in terms of large numbers and of peaceful conduct. But if its purpose was to influence the House of Lords as well as to protect the image of the council, it had no opportunity to do any good. On the very evening of the meeting, the government was defeated on a motion by Lord Lyndhurst to postpone consideration of the disfranchising clauses of the bill. The next day Grey went to Windsor with the cabinet's ultimatum for power to create peers. The king asked for a night to consider, but the outcome was foregone, and on May 9 he accepted the ministers' resignations. The country received the news of the resignations the following day, uniformly with intense, spontaneous anger.

It was early in the morning when the London newspapers bearing the tidings arrived in Birmingham. Quickly the word of Grey's resignation spread. By nine o'clock members of the union had started to gather at their headquarters at Great Charles Street, and soon afterward the building was filled and hundreds of persons stood in the street outside. Attwood was not yet present, for his home was at Harborne about four miles away, but at eleven o'clock he appeared, looking alarmed and dejected. Scarcely had he taken the chair when Parkes led a large deputation into the council chamber and presented him with a statement freshly signed by five hundred professional and mercantile men. They hitherto had kept aloof from the union, they said, but now they were prepared to join and to lend their support to the council. The delighted Attwood praised their "patriotism" and suggested that the statement and names be printed and circulated through-

out the town, to show that a true union of the classes was now
occurring. Also, he recommended that the members of the union
cease to wear the union medal, which contained an image of the
crown that had failed them. Meanwhile, the crowd in the street
had grown larger and the speakers could no longer ignore its
presence, whereupon Salt and Pare moved that the council meet
the inhabitants of the city at Newhall Hill that afternoon to determine what measures to take during the crisis. The motion passed
and the leaders repaired to a private room to prepare for the
meeting.[26]

But what could they propose? The crisis clearly was dissolving
the class distinctions along which the local politics had operated
until now. Not only were the business and professional men grav-
itating to the union for protection, but also there was a danger
that if the council failed to arrive at some clear policy immediately, the shopkeepers and workers would desert the union for
the leadership of the more radical elements in town. Already
some of the shopkeepers were displaying in their windows placards printed by Russell which proclaimed, "No Taxes Paid Here
Until the Reform Bill Is Passed." A few of the councilmen acknowledged the mood of the members and wanted some decisive
action, such as a refusal to pay taxes, a run on the banks (to
which the chairman could hardly agree), or even physical resistance. But, according to Parkes, who was present along with
others of the new upper middle-class allies of the council,
Attwood and the rest deprecated all such propositions. They
argued that even if the king had fallen victim to evil advisers, the
House of Commons remained on the side of the people and
retained the power to prevent the existence of a Tory government. The union therefore must petition that House to use all of
its power to return Grey to office and to get the bill passed. In the
meanwhile the danger of armed action by the boroughmongers,
long feared by the council, seemingly had increased, and thus the
resolutions included a warning to the Commons that in this crisis
the whole of the people of England might soon think it necessary
to have arms for the defense of their lives and property. The
motion apparently was not so much a threat as it was an intimation that this illegal action, ruled out the previous November,

might be forced upon political unions and other bodies of reformers by their concern for their own personal safety.

The meeting at Newhall Hill got off to a poor start, but eventually it went according to plan. Placards had announced the event, and an officially estimated 100,000 persons deserted their shops and homes to respond. Russell reported that the proportion of men and youths was as high as two-thirds of the total. A few banners decorated the scene, but the holiday spirit characteristic of the two previous meetings was absent. Edmonds's appeal for patience at the start of the proceedings drew shouts of disapproval, and Attwood caused great confusion when he rose and assured his excited hearers that "all things are going on as well as they ought to be expected to go." But the banker soon earned cheers when he explained that his optimism was based upon the fact that hundreds of respectable men had joined the union that morning. He was additionally reassured of the crowd's support when he referred to the possibility that a new government might kidnap him and he was answered with a great chorus of voices crying "No, no!" The resolutions and petition then passed amid loud applause.

The meeting over and the petition engrossed, a deputation consisting of Scholefield, Parkes, and John Green (a banker and leader of the Dissenters, and, like Parkes, a new member of the union) left for London in a chaise-and-four to deliver the document to O'Connell for presentation to the House of Commons. The choice of the three men—two of whom were not Ultra-Tories—reflected the sudden merging of forces during the crisis, but it also indicated more. There now was an urgent need for contact with the government and with moderate leaders outside of Birmingham, something Attwood had neglected to this point. Each of the three men apparently was selected because he personally was acquainted with some of the mnisters; in addition, the trio was instructed to communicate with the "friends of Reform" in London and to report back to the council as early as possible. After seeing the deputation off, the council had then to try to conceal from the members their private fears as they waited for further developments. All night the death bells tolled from various churches in the city. The next morning, however, there arrived unexpected tidings by the *Sun* express from London: the House of Commons had reacted at once to the resignations and had voted 288 to 208 in favor of a motion by Lord Ebrington affirming their unaltered confidence in the old government. Immediately the bells changed to joyous peals and crowds gathered around the newsoffices to learn of the improved prospects for peaceful reform. The alarm felt during the preceding day abated rapidly.

During the day Attwood and his associates found much to do locally. The leaders of most of the unions around Birmingham came to confer with them and to offer assistance; the council encouraged these supporters to stage meetings in their own towns. The clerks at the union office continued to enroll new members, reportedly almost two thousand by the end of the day. By midday the council had decided to address the king. They were far too royalist to cast lightly aside an attachment which they believed had accomplished so much, and there always was hope that William might be rescued from the oligarchs who had captured him. The address appealed, "We respectfully implore your Majesty, as the father of your people, to raise them from the depth of despair, to call to the Royal Councils those Ministers in whom only they can place confidence . . . " The document was signed by all of the councilmen and sent off to Lord Melbourne for presentation to the king.[27] After that, the council could do little but to await results.

In the meantime the members of the deputation to London carried out their assignments. They delivered a report of the Newhall Hill meeting to the newspapers and they gave the petition to O'Connell for presentation to the House of Commons. Since the House already had voted its unaltered support of the Grey ministry, the latter action had lost much of its intended importance. The deputation found the city alive to the indignation in the country over the resignation of Grey and properly attentive to them as representatives of the fourth city and the largest meetings in England. The Whiggish Scholefield soon arranged for an interview between himself and Grey. At Parkes's suggestion all three men also conferred with Place, and they attended reform meetings of the Livery at the Guildhall and of the inhabitants of Westminster at the Crown and Anchor, where they were received favorably.[28] No reliable record exists of their communicating with anyone other than these middle-class reformers or of their doing more than learning the Londoners' sentiments concerning the crisis. Place's written account in later years about his having plotted revolution with the Birmingham deputation is highly improbable and likely reflected nothing more than some agitated talk between himself and Parkes, both of whom were given to such activity.[29] Far from their agreeing that Birmingham would be the first to hoist the standard of revolt, as Place claimed, the council by reason both of temperament and of concern for property would have been the last body to assent unconditionally to such a proposition.

A new development, much dreaded by the council, occurred on May 12 and became known in Birmingham on Sunday, the 13th: the king had commissioned the Duke of Wellington to form a government on the basis of a compromise reform bill. A few hours following the receipt of this news, Scholefield returned from London with word that Grey had said that there was nothing to be done but to keep the people quiet and permit the Duke to introduce his own plan of reform. The next morning Scholefield related the details of his interview to the full council and to a gallery packed with members. Outside in the town, the shop-keepers were in a fever of excitement and were complaining of a lack of leadership; some observers believed that they were pre-pared on their own to refuse taxes. Adding to the uncertainty was a run on the savings banks begun by some jittery depositors. But what could the leaders of the union advise now? Apparently none of them advocated illegal resistance of any sort, lest he invite the arrest of the whole council—an occurrence which, one of the new members reported, "is looked upon as a probable measure." Attwood in particular remained determined to follow a course of moral action and to keep strictly within the law, and he and other speakers successfully argued against any precipitate action.[30]

At length the council decided to issue a "Solemn Declaration" that the people would never cease to use all constitutional means to induce the king to reject Wellington and recall Grey and get the great bill of reform passed into law.[31] All of the nation's reformers, including those in Parliament, would be invited to sign the manifesto—one estimate was that four million people would do so—and the Duke of Norfolk would be asked to present it to the king "as a great national document." At first it was intended that the reformers of each place should return to the council a copy of the Declaration with signatures attached, but in the interest of haste it was decided later that they would be asked instead to send to the *Journal* or to the London newspapers a certified statement of the number who had signed. The council drew up the Declaration and they and some of their new allies signed it on May 14, but the printing and distribution of it was delayed so that lawyers might first be consulted concerning the absolute legality of the proceeding. This was done, and the following afternoon copies of the document were displayed in Birmingham and were sent off by express to all parts of the United Kingdom.

Again there was the prospect of an agonizing wait for further news. The possibility of violence loomed from every direction, for on one hand the council feared that the Duke would resort instantly to repressive measures, and on the other there was danger because, as a reporter put it, "the low people in the streets at night utter the most horrid imprecations against the King, the Queen, and the Duke of Wellington." Attwood's uneasiness was evident from the fact that he sent for his brother Charles, chairman of the Northern Political Union at Newcastle, to come and be with him during the crisis. Meanwhile the affairs of the union occupied him and the council. Although a group of Whigs and Dissenters refused to sign the Solemn Declaration and circulated a competitive "Solemn League and Covenant," the effort smacked of petty politics at an inopportune time; the union seemed to offer the clearest alternative to civil strife, and so the three clerks at the union office continued to labor at registering the names of new members. As many as 2,000 additional men joined on the 14th alone.[32] There was also the task of informing the neighboring unions about the council's decisions and of soliciting their support. Salt and McDonnell, for example, attended a meeting convened by the union at Worcester and both men commented that it was their third such engagement of the day.[33]

Once more welcome news arrived with unexpected promptness. On the same day that the council had drawn up their Solemn Declaration, the House of Commons had approved a motion by Ebrington asserting that it would never accept a reform bill from the Duke of Wellington. The speeches during the debate were so venomous that a number of Wellington's supporters afterward went to him and told him that no Tory ministers could face the House. By this time the Duke had grown discouraged over his inability to recruit men for a new government, and he now faced up to the inevitable. The next day he went to the king and told him that he had failed, leaving William no choice but to recall Grey to office. It was this news that Parkes brought from London at six o'clock on the morning of May 16 and that touched off demonstrations of joy and relief equaling in intensity the tension which was dispelled.

Parkes first sought out Jones, who hurried off to get the church bells clamming. After arranging for expresses to take the tidings to all the towns nearby, Parkes set out for Attwood's residence at Harborne. When he arrived there about 7:30 he found guards behind the shrubbery around the house—villagers, he believed, but union members, it was later reported. "Attwood was in bed," Parkes wrote a friend a few days later, "his whole family really expecting warrants for high treason or sedition. I need not tell you what were the grateful sensations of the whole family, or the tears of the women."[34] Later a half dozen of the councilmen arrived and joined "the father of the unions" in a triumphal procession back into Birmingham. After parading the principal streets they arrived at Newhall Hill, where a gathering estimated variously between 40,000 and 80,000 persons voted approval of resolutions and memorials of thanks to Grey and to the reformers in Parliament and London. The leaders of the union were all deeply moved by the turn of events; Edmonds's eyes were red with weeping and he could hardly speak. Attwood had a young Unitarian minister who had just joined the union lead the gathering in a prayer of thanksgiving for the deliverance which they had had from the threat of revolution. Then the chairman made a speech in which he expressed his belief that the union had acted as God's principal agent. "I cannot but express the great delight I feel," he declared, "in Birmingham having been mainly instrumental in the accomplishment of this glorious consummation"; he had told them that Grey would be restored to office, and "by your unparalleled patience and your virtue, I have been enabled to fulfill my promise." That evening a deputation appointed by

Attwood on the authority of the meeting left in triumph for London to deliver engrossed copies of the resolutions and memorials to the parties concerned.[35]

It was impossible that Attwood and his associates should not misinterpret their role in the recent events. Their version of things quickly emerged, and it was wholly in keeping with their unorthodox view of politics. Perhaps it was expressed best in the first resolution submitted to the meeting, in which they happily anticipated "the complete emancipation of his Majesty from the snares and wicked devices of base, evil-minded, and desperate councillors." A moral struggle centering on the throne, in short, and one that had been won, as before, by the union through its pronouncements. It mattered little that the House of Commons had acted before the Birmingham petition had arrived, that the king had refused to receive the address sent to him,[36] and that Wellington had given up before the Solemn Declaration could be signed by anybody. It simply made sense that the ones who spoke for the combined middle and lower classes of the nation must have brought it off once more. "Our declaration against the Duke," Attwood wrote unequivocally, "has done the business."[37] There existed among the council, to be sure, an awareness of the countless angry meetings held elsewhere in the country, but these seemed merely a backdrop to their own addresses and declarations. The council after all had called for such meetings, had they not? Therefore it was not possible for Attwood and his friends to see themselves as others now saw them. There was a genuine admiration in the country, and especially in London, for the skillful manner in which Attwood had managed the turbulent spirits in his union and had staged the great meetings at Birmingham. To some extent the union had become associated in the minds of reformers everywhere with the possibility and hope of peaceful reform, with the tactic of pressure combined with restraint. The enthusiastic compliments paid to the council on this occasion of rejoicing simply reflected this appreciation for Birmingham's contribution to the general cause; to the council, on the other hand, the words of praise confirmed their own belief that the union virtually alone had accomplished the deliverance of the nation.

The reception given the deputation in London was highly flattering. Dinner invitations came from various Radical leaders, and Attwood at length wrote to his wife, "If we do not leave London shortly, we shall have more to fear from the Dinners, than from the Barricades & Cannon Balls."[38] Other leaders of the union soon came down to share in the festivities, including Muntz, who had re-joined the council during the crisis and who now was added officially to the deputation. Lords Grey and Holland granted several of the councilmen an interview so that they might present the memorial that the meeting had voted to the prime minister. The *Journal* reported that the two ministers received them with every mark of attention and respect, a misleading courteousness, for the next day Grey told a confidant about "how annoyed he was to see them come with their ribbons and badges, knowing the misrepresentation that would be made of his reception of them in that character."[39] The high point of the activities in the metropolis came on May 23, when the Corporation of London received the vote of thanks of the Birmingham meeting and in turn presented Attwood with the freedom of the city and gave a splendid banquet at the Mansion House for the visitors. The attention thoroughly delighted the council, but by this time Attwood may have been sincere when he wrote that he and Bosco were "tired to death with honours & dinners."[40]

One brief emergency intruded into the celebrations. The king had agreed to create peers *if necessary* to pass the bill. At the same time he had sought promises from the Duke and other antagonists of the measure that they would publicly declare an end to their opposition, thus obviating the need for a creation. Wellington seemed prepared to do so, but on the evening of May 17 he and his followers stalked out of the House of Lords without making the declaration, prompting Grey to demand an unconditional pledge from William on the matter. The new impasse created alarm among reformers far exceeding the actual seriousness of the situation. Attwood began talking of a gigantic meeting of one million people to join him at Hampstead Heath in "a grand exhibition" of reform feeling.[41] How far he got in the matter is uncertain. The Westminster reformers evidently had no serious part in the proposal, for the council of the National Union recently had voted against a unified meeting of London unions there and Place made no mention of such a project in his papers. Place instead was calling for a run on gold, the mere threat of which, he boasted, had worked out the reformation thus far and would soon settle the matter for good.[42]

The alternative path for Attwood was cooperation with the working-class radicals, and he now abandoned his opposition to them sufficiently to ask Dr. Wade to join the National Union of the Working Classes, which included the remnants of the old Metropolitan Union, and to suggest to them the possibility of the project. The vicar was the one man on the council extremist enough for the assignment—a few days earlier he had called the antireformist bishops "bare assed monkeys climbing up poles"—but whether he could have negotiated arrangements for the Hampstead Heath meeting without significant concessions to radicalism is doubtful.[43] In any case, the king on the 18th conceded to Grey the power the cabinet had demanded and simultaneously he wrote the Tory peers that they had to choose between the bill with an addition to the peerage or the bill without it. The hostilities ceased. For Attwood, this dying kick of the boroughmongers merely confirmed the decisiveness of the union's verdict over them. "Our Meetings in Birmingham," he wrote the next day, "have been like claps of thunder bursting over the heads of our enemies, & our Declaration against the D. of Wellington has sealed the doom of his party for ever."

Most important, the passage of the reform bill now opened the way to still greater things. There yet remained the "master evil," Peel's Currency Act of 1819. To the banker's delight, he was invited to return to London in a few days and testify before a parliamentary committee on the subject. In exultation he wrote to his wife, "The Banking Com[mitt]ee seems likely to fall into my hands. In this case, you will see, my Dear, that I shall have been a great instrument in giving Liberty, Prosperity & *Virtue* to a distressed & oppressed people."[44]

THOMAS ATTWOOD. The picture is from a painting by G. Sharples.

JOSHUA SCHOLEFIELD

THOMAS C. SALT. From *The Charter*.

GEORGE F. MUNTZ. From the *Illustrated London News.*

GEORGE EDMONDS

DR. ARTHUR WADE

CHAPTER V

Postlude to Parliamentary Reform

July 1832–June 1834

ON MAY 28, 1832, Attwood returned to Birmingham, in his words, "bearing my blushing honours thick upon me."[1] The councilmen who had remained behind arranged a triumphal entry for him and the deputation. A diarist of the period recorded that there were "thousands of banners and flags waving in all directions; bells ringing, trumpets sounding, balloons flying, guns firing, people shouting, and bands playing; every window and door, and even the housetops, crowded with human beings saluting the procession with the most deafening cheers." Another eyewitness wrote that the crowd pressed so hard about Attwood's carriage that they broke the pole and harness, whereupon they removed the horses and pushed the vehicle up New Street to the Hen and Chickens Hotel.[2] There the banker made a speech from the portico in which he rejoiced that "the final knell of despotism has tolled—the night of our misery is passing away—the bright day of our liberty and our happiness is beginning to dawn."[3] Other thousands awaited the procession farther along the announced route, but it was growing dark and they were disappointed.

The euphoria of the council continued for some days. The artist Benjamin Haydon, who was engaged in sketching portraits of the council for a painting of the May 16 meeting, wrote that "they have been so excited lately they are absolutely languid in conversation. But they are high in feeling—*Roman* quite—and will be immortal in their great struggle."

Already a process of legend-making had set in. Haydon quoted Jones as saying that he had told the tax collector who had called during the crisis, "If you dare, Sir, to call again, I'll have you nailed by the ear to my door, with a placard on your breast saying who you are!"[4] Other stories related how warrants actually had been made out for the arrest of the union leaders but remained unsigned in the Home Office; how the government had offered Attwood an enormous cash bribe or a place in the ministry during both the October and the May crises; and how the soldiers stationed in the Birmingham barracks had spent three days sharpening their swords. The paraphernalia of the great victory also grew steadily. There were new union medals on which the image of the chairman replaced that of the crown (although the old ones soon became acceptable again); there were many pictures of Attwood, as well as pipes and beer mugs fashioned in his image; and there were blue garters for the ladies inscribed with the words "Attwood forever!" Everywhere that the banker went in the city he was hailed as the savior of the country. On June 29, he and Scholefield formally announced their candidacy for the representation of the borough in Parliament.[5] It was assumed that nobody would be so mad as to contest them for the votes of the applauding, newly enfranchised shopkeepers.

Almost without realizing it the council got themselves involved in a flurry of new agitation, a step they took seemingly unaware of its implications for their future standing in the country. During the struggle for parliamentary reform the union had been one of a multitude of bodies demanding the bill, and the council had consistently backed the government as the best means of achieving success. Birmingham's victories therefore were indistinguishable from the nation's and the government's victories, and not until the council undertook projects on their own and in opposition to the ministers could observers determine the union's true national influence. The start of fresh agitation opened the way at once to such an evaluation.

The focus of the campaign was upon Ireland. Early in the agitation for reform the council had addressed the Irish people and had urged them to postpone their efforts to get a repeal of the Act of Union and to join the people of England in seeking a reform of Parliament. Under O'Connell's leadership this was done. Now that the English reform bill had become law, O'Connell began to agitate against the Irish reform bill, contending that it was inferior to the English and Scottish measures. The council could hardly ignore the complaints. Indeed, William Cobbett would not let them, for, continuing his tirade against the union as an alleged tool of the government, he pointed to the Irish issue among others as a test of the council's independence. On June 12, the council adopted a petition to Parliament calling for a stronger bill for Ireland, and the following week they summoned the inhabitants of the town to meet at Newhall Hill on June 25 to reenforce their demand. Haynes voiced their unanimous sentiment when he declared that "he should blush to occupy a seat at that council, if they consented whilst English liberty was welcomed by Mr. Attwood as a bridegroom, to see Irish freedom mourned by Mr. O'Connell as a widower." They all agreed that the people of England looked to them as leaders and that when the fiat went forth from the union it would be heeded.[6]

The meeting was held, but had no effect in the country or in Parliament. The Irish reform bill passed without the slightest difficulty. The legislators seemed oblivious to the fact that a Newhall Hill meeting had tried to flag them down, and their inattention was shared fully by the country. *The Times* and the *Morning Chronicle* did not print a line of the report sent to them, and very few places held meetings to back the council. Even the people of Birmingham may have disappointed the unionists on this occasion, for the *Proceedings* of the meeting oddly omitted any estimate of attendance. The endeavor, in sum, was a complete failure.

At this point inherent weaknesses in the union became painfully apparent, weaknesses that had been disregarded during the heady days of the agitation for parliamentary reform. The union in fact was grounded on a political myth, on the fiction that it had accomplished the great victory of 1830–1832 by uniting the middle and working classes and leading them in a

95

moral confrontation with evil monetary and boroughmongering conspirators. The society in this regard was not unique: political myths were part of the nineteenth-century British scene, and though they might have national connotations, they were begun and nurtured by specific local situations. They could be particularly strong in places such as Birmingham, where provincialism and peculiar religious doctrines sheltered and stimulated them. Of course they were most likely to spread to places with similar conditions. Sometimes the myth pitted a vague leadership (such as a General Ludd or a Captain Swing) against a specific enemy; in other cases, as at Birmingham, a specific leadership acted against a vague enemy; but both varieties relied upon unconventional tactics such as violence or moral force. The movements based upon the myths promised relief locally or regionally to an oppressed or declining group which seemingly had little hope of winning a place in the existing society. Yet there was an important catch: the political myth was a delicate fabrication, a faith capable of turning political peasants and children into crusaders, but also which was apt to collapse when confronted with problems and enemies in a harsh world. The crisis was most damaging when it was experienced locally, when practical difficulties and unfulfilled promises could erode the beliefs that had created and sustained the fable. This erosion now beset the unionist myth at Birmingham.

One facet of the developing crisis in the union's position was the collapse of the council's contention that dedication to a great cause enabled them to transcend practical problems and personal differences. The council, for example, had talked little of finances, yet there continually had existed an acute shortage of funds. In the first six months of operation the council had raised only £325; the amount collected the next year, including the nonprofit sale of medals, was £809, and for the following year, ending in July 1832, it was about £1,400.[7] During the May 1832 crisis Parkes wrote that the union's finances were *"in extremis."*[8] The situation grew worse after the passage of the reform bill, for the total income during the next two years apparently came to less than £600. One of the councilmen in 1837 stated that the whole amount raised for the

purposes of the union from the beginning through 1834 was
only £3,108, and, more surprising, that of this amount not
more than £800 was collected from the working men.[9] Since
there were about 20,000 men enrolled in the union in 1833,
including 7,000 who joined in May 1832, and since only 500
persons were pledged to more than the minimum subscription,[10] the above figure would indicate that prior to the passage
of the reform bill probably no more than one-fourth of the
members paid their penny-a-week dues, and thereafter no
more than one-tenth. The few who paid did so reluctantly, for
the union's leaders later admitted that half of the income from
these subscribers went to pay the collectors.

The harshest interpretation of members' avoidance of dues
was that expressed by the antiunionist *Argus*, which called
them "a ragged set" who "will applaud, yell, and break windows, for their oily-tongued leaders; but as to putting their
hands in their pockets to support them—'I beg you won't mention it.' "[11] Some friends of the council bitterly shared this
view. A fairer interpretation, however, is that the council virtually ensured such indifference to dues by the authoritarian
way they conducted the union. The members permitted the
council almost unlimited control of the organization, but in turn
they expected them to be largely self-supporting. The resulting
paucity of income was not very damaging during the agitation
for the reform bill because the entire country already was
active and advice in the form of addresses was cheap. Now,
with the failure of their new campaign, the lack of finances
was keenly felt.

A second weakness of the union threatened to break it up
before insolvency could end it: the conflicting philosophies and
temperaments of the councilmen, a source of divisive irritation
which already had flared repeatedly. The fundamental problem
was that Attwood's currency faction desired political changes
sufficient only to effect monetary ones, whereas the Radicals
advocated modification of the political system as a goal in
itself. The question bound to arise after May 1832 was whether
the council should concentrate on the currency or should pursue other objectives, including further steps toward democracy.
Complicating the matter were numerous personal

antagonisms among the councilmen, differences that barely had been suppressed during the drive for the reform bill and that, with the removal of this restraint, quickly found expression. The result of all of these frictions, philosophical and personal, was a series of damaging, public squabbles that stretched throughout the remainder of the year.

In the most publicized of the quarrels Attwood himself exchanged harsh words with his associates. At the banker's prompting the council had adopted a declaration to the electors of the country urging them to require pledges on all important issues from the candidates for Parliament. Attwood, of course, had in mind the currency question in pressing the matter. But the Radicals on the council drew up a list of other issues and in the interest of impartiality they insisted that the local candidates, Attwood and Scholefield, must undergo questioning on them. To their surprise Attwood expressed his "utter disgust" over their action, which he termed as unnecessary as "gilding refined gold, painting the lily, and perfuming the violet." "It showed a mean dastardly suspicion," he said, and "clearly proved that there was treachery in the camp." The outcome was that a majority of the council timidly backed down and agreed that the chairman need not pledge himself on anything other than the relief of distress. But several councilmen used the occasion to resign. Simultaneously, Scholefield submitted his resignation in the aftermath of an altercation with Edmonds over who should be the unionist candidate for Parliament along with Attwood.[12]

Despite this internecine brawling and the continued letdown in morale after their defeat on the Irish question, the council had to prepare for the annual meeting of the union in July. At a session on the 17th the disparate factions among them finally began to find common cause in the distress which they agreed existed undiminished in Birmingham. Salt said that only the hope which the people still placed in the council kept the sufferers from giving themselves up to wild despair, and he suggested that the unionists prove the existence of hardship to the rest of the country by getting local manufacturers and tradesmen to sign a declaration of facts. Pare and McDonnell agreed to the strategy but proposed instead that they go to the working classes. Salt answered that it had to be the middle classes, to show that the distress "was rapidly reaching the vitals." Finally Muntz resolved the dispute by suggesting that they prepare separate documents and solicit the signatures of both working and middle classes. Next, the council proceeded to the problem of what remedies to stress. The logical solution was to advocate a joint program of currency revision and other reforms, and this tentatively was agreed upon, although the Radical measures were not specified and were to follow later.[13] A modicum of harmony temporarily returned to the council.

More damaging than these internal problems and quarrels, harmful though they proved to be, was the erosion of the utopian component of the unionist myth. Perhaps the most frequently repeated part of the unionist vision was the promise by Attwood's faction that unlimited prosperity and happiness would result from the victory over the boroughmongers. The Ultra-Tories' success in forcing the Radicals on the council to give currency reform first consideration meant that they could now deliver on their pledges. The action centered on forcing the ministers to acknowlege the nation's great debt to the Birmingham union and to repay it by granting monetary reform. To this end, the council had the annual business meeting of the union endorse their demand for cheap currency, and on August 22 they instructed a deputation to deliver the document to the prime minister. Salt enthusiastically proclaimed once more the opening of the "second campaign" of the union, and he urged the deputation to tell Grey that no minister would be allowed to rule in England who allowed the present system of fraud and folly to continue.[14] Meanwhile, Attwood, already in London, had appeared at last before the banking committee, and although he found not a single friend of cheap money on it (his brother Matthias was sick and absent) he believed that Althorp and Grey at last had come around to his opinions. A month later he still was optimistic that he and the council had managed to influence the ministers, and he wrote his wife, "Now, if I succeed in getting the Currency rectified, I am afraid it will make you proud. Only think what a fine thing it will be to have assisted, first in obtaining *Liberty*, second, in preventing *Anarchy*, third, in restoring *Prosperity!*"[15]

He and Jones had just evidenced their zeal on the question by publicly debating with Cobbett the merits of paper money as against equitable adjustment, a debate in which Attwood spoke for six and a half hours.[16] A few days later, nevertheless, the currency faction's hopes for governmental adoption of their ideas were rudely dashed. Attwood sent Grey a printed report of his debate with Cobbett, and the prime minister without bothering to read it replied that "I much fear that your opinions & mine will not agree as to the nature of the remedy to which you look for the relief of the existing distress."[17] The rebuff meant that the council now had little choice but to await the works of the reformed House of Commons. Perhaps Attwood and Scholefield as M.P.s could influence it. In the interval utopia would have to be postponed.

During these months another part of the myth also was collapsing, the dogma that the union had effected a true union of classes in Britain. The fallacy to which Attwood and his followers subscribed was that their predictions of economic distress preceding the recession of 1829 and their subsequent support of the reform bill with the largest meetings in England had made them the ongoing spokesmen for all the classes in the kingdom who had feared hardship or who had desired reform. The assumption simply was not true, and nationally the council's perennial themes of conspiracy and imminent disaster sounded bizarre to the middle classes following the victory of 1832. As for the lower classes, the refusal of the council to espouse democracy left the "low radical" leaders firmly in command in that quarter. The radical chieftains saw no need for guidance from or for gratitude to the council; far from giving Attwood credit for having gained the passage of reform, they themselves accepted responsibility for that event. Cobbett, for example, wrote that he personally had "done more in making a reform than any other thousand men in England."[18] Many radicals continued to accuse the council of truckling to the ministers. Nor did political unions outside of the Midlands acknowledge any continuing obligation to the "parent union." In the one instance in which the council sought to exercise an influence upon the 1832 elections outside of Warwickshire—a circular letter to the electors of Hull supporting the candidacy of Matthew D. Hill, son of Attwood's election manager and a moderate—they received a curt letter from the Hull and Sculcoates Political Union denouncing them for their "thoughtless and mischievous interference."[19]

Even in Birmingham things quickly returned to their former state. Most of the five hundred mercantile and professional men who had joined the union now left it, and some of them, including Parkes and Green, went so far as to advertise their resignations. To these seceders, the council once more became the much-ridiculed "Brummagem legislature" elected by "Attwood's scum," an absurd body which supposed that their public-house talk about issues had serious consequences for the nation. Perhaps their departure was to be expected. What was unanticipated was the defection of the shopkeepers from the activities of the union. Almost at once the council had to recognize the altered status of the shopkeepers: the council's declaration of the "middle classes" on distress included "the tradesmen" for the first time with the manufacturers and merchants, a move made necessary, McDonnell observed, because the shopkeepers no longer identified with the workers on the question of distress. In the squabble over pledges, Attwood said that he was not certain that the new voters were favorable to radical measures, and that it was foolish to offend them.[20] The Radicals simultaneously marked the division in the ranks of the unionists by organizing meetings of "non-electors" to back their own demands. By 1834 the editor of the *Journal* was ready to write off the shopkeepers entirely, declaring that they were "in the open possession of the great capitalists" on political matters.[21] The judgment was too harsh, for the shopkeepers of Birmingham proved loyal to Attwood in the elections; their reluctance was to join the workers in unionist campaigns for further reforms. Their tacit departure left only the workers as the real constituency of the union, and there were indications that Attwood could no longer rely upon the laborers themselves if his instructions conflicted with those given by the new trade unions appearing in the city.

Further resignations from the council took place during these months, undoubtedly caused in part by the prolonged feuding among the leaders. By the time of the general meeting in 1833, only fourteen of the original thirty-six members of the council remained, and only eighteen of the thirty additions made through November 1831. The departing members included "8 leading middle men" who had helped support the union financially and who according to Parkes recently had tired of the society.[22] Among less prosperous but more conspicuous leaders lost to the council were Parkin and Weston, refused reelection at the general meeting in 1832 for supporting hard money and church rates; Haynes, who left Birmingham in the fall of 1832, evidently under some financial cloud; and McDonnell, who resigned early in 1833 after refusing to pay a debt which he had incurred for the union by an unauthorized public entry given O'Connell. Newcomers took their places, of course, the most important of whom was John Powell, a writing clerk, radical Owenite Co-operative organizer, and former secretary of the shareholders of the now defunct *Midland Representative*. But the union unquestionably was hurt by the attrition in the ranks of the old council. Attwood himself suspected that some subversive work by the reviving oligarchs was involved: "In less than three years," he said, the council "had accomplished the greatest political change recorded in the history of the world"; only an enemy of the people could seek to divide such a body.[23]

It obviously was a salutary move when the council recessed for the final five weeks of 1832. The explanation offered was that the councilmen wanted time to assist their chairman and former deputy chairman in the forthcoming parliamentary election, but a major factor must have been the need to let their numerous bruises mend. The local election required little of their attention. The nonunionist radicals and Conservatives, though they talked of opposition, prudently allowed Attwood and Scholefield to run uncontested and to become the first representatives of Birmingham to the House of Commons.

A renewed attempt by the council to generate national agitation by moral confrontation got under way in February 1833, a further test of the "moral power" aspect of the unionist myth. Several things induced the fresh effort. The most publicized of them was a series of "farewell addresses" given by Attwood prior to his leaving for London to begin his parliamentary duties. The

banker warned that the union's work was only half done and that
a yet more terrible crisis was approaching as a result of the continued control of the economy by the wicked oligarchy. There
were related political dangers also, for the Whigs, who so
recently had sided with the people against the oligarchs, showed
signs of deserting the popular cause. Even though the gaol, the
halter, and the block might still await the council, Attwood said,
they must at once prepare themselves for further moral battle;
they had his promise that he would return in a crisis to share
whatever fate befell them.[24]

Interestingly enough, Attwood's departure for London in itself
furthered the movement toward fresh agitation. Whatever veiled
threats his words might contain, the chairman was extremely
cautious by nature, and so his going was the removal of a
restraining hand. Muntz as deputy chairman henceforth was to
preside over the council, and in contrast to Attwood the metal
roller was both short-tempered and impulsive. His aggressive
style was especially influential because the other leaders of the
council likewise seemed prepared for action, perhaps because it
was clear to most of them that as outsiders in politics they had no
pretense of a large audience or of power apart from an active
union.

It followed that Muntz and his associates were not likely to give
the remodeled Parliament and the ministers who had sponsored
its reform a very extended trial. Indeed, they found the Speech
from the Throne to the initial session of the legislature "most
unacceptable." Muntz asserted that in omitting any reference to
distress the ministers were either "extremely ignorant, or extremely criminal"; it did not appear, he said, that they were prepared either to lift up the people's means or to reduce their bur-
dens. Other councilmen concurred, and affirmed that the
standard of the union must again be unfurled. To get their
"second campaign" started, on February 19 the council decided
upon a public meeting to back three combined Ultra-Tory and
Radical measures: (1) a repeal of all taxes that pressed unfairly
upon the industrious classes, plus "an investigation into the
cause of distress" (currency reform), (2) a repeal of taxes on
knowledge, and (3) an abandonment of the government's proposed bill to pacify Ireland. All three measures were to be em-

bodied in petitions to the House of Commons, and reformers everywhere were to be urged to meet and agitate for them. Salt seemed to speak the sentiments of the entire council when he proclaimed that the people of England "would soon hear an old and accustomed voice, and he was confident that an appeal from the Birmingham Union would not be disregarded, but would meet with a hearty response from every part of the kingdom."[25]

The meeting was held at Beardsworth's on February 25, 1833. Several of the councilmen had wanted a Newhall Hill affair, but Bosco Attwood had persuaded them that the need for haste—the Irish bill would be before the House in a few days—and the risk of unfavorable weather dictated otherwise. For some reason, perhaps budgetary, none of the usual means of excitement was employed. The unionists ignored their previous estimates of the capacity of the Repository and reported that 12,000 or more persons attended and "crowded the building to excess"; the Tory press insisted that this figure was grossly exaggerated.[26] The theme of the meeting was that Lord Grey's government was no better than its predecessors had been—Whig thieves in the night being as bad as Tory barefaced highwaymen—and therefore the council could not in good conscience remain silent.

But if the purpose of the meeting was to call attention to the "true character" of the ministry, it was an unqualified failure. Most of the country took no notice of the indictment, and the few observers who did note it seemed not to care. None of the principal London newspapers printed a line of the report sent to them. Very few meetings were held to back the council, even in the Midlands, and most observers evidently shared the *Manchester Guardian's* view that the terrible crisis about which Attwood and his friends currently talked was the strong likelihood that the nation's leaders would reject their "currency nostrums."[27] Meanwhile, in Parliament the Irish Coercion bill passed unimpeded.

The defeat suffered by the council in their role as "national leaders" was followed by one inflicted personally upon their representative in Parliament. Attwood looked to the new House of Commons to sanction the union's quest for utopian prosperity, and thus one of his first acts as an M.P. was to move for a select committee to inquire into the causes of distress. The malady which he suspected and the medicine which he was eager to prescribe already were well known, and so the motion was a legislative test of his monetary views. Attwood should have anticipated the outcome, for Charles Western, a long-time parliamentary opponent of hard money, wrote him in January that the ministers had given no thought to the state of the currency and that the House was not likely to pay much attention to a newcomer. Nevertheless, Attwood was confident enough to write Bosco, "I think I shall succeed."[28] When the motion came to a vote in March, the banker in an impassioned speech told the House that "there were, at this moment, millions of families in the United Kingdom who hourly die many deaths, who envy the victims of broken hearts that have died before them, and who lived, as it were, sowing in sorrow, and reaping only ruin as the reward of their anxiety and toil"; those who had "not yet drunk of the bitter cup," he said, were "waiting in alarm the coming of the threatened storm." The government refused to support the motion, however, and the House rejected it.[29] To make matters worse, several of the London newspapers treated the affair as a joke and amused themselves at Attwood's expense. *The Times* managed to be particularly irritating by dubbing him the "Brummagem Hampden," and although the new M.P. wrote the customary angry reply to the editor his protest served merely to prolong the ridicule.[30]

Undeniably, the council now were in a difficult position. They had presented the ministers with something like an ultimatum to change direction, only to be disregarded by everybody. Only two further courses therefore remained open to the Birmingham leaders: they either had to find some way at once to demonstrate conclusively their national influence, or else admit to political impotency. Illusions of power die hard, and after some uncertainty the council began to recover their spirits. The true moral power of the union had been manifested in 1831 and 1832 by *regional* meetings held at Birmingham, and these were yet to be tried against the Whigs. At a session at the end of March, Salt got shouts of approval from the gallery when he told his fellow councilmen that they had no choice but to call for addresses to the king from all parts of the nation, praying him to dismiss his ministers forthwith. The other speakers agreed that the government by its "infamous conduct" had proved itself unworthy of the confidence of the council and of the country, and therefore, as Muntz announced amid great applause, the sooner the Grey ministry "gave place to abler and honester men the better." The same moral power that twice had driven Wellington from office was to be unleashed against the Whigs. The next month the council announced their intention to hold a great regional meeting at Newhall Hill. An unanswered question was whether Attwood would lend his support, for during a visit home two weeks earlier the chairman had recommended to the council patience and caution. But this was before further parliamentary rebuffs on the subject of the currency, and upon being consulted Attwood approved of their course.[31]

Numerous preparations had to be made for the Newhall Hill meeting, set for May 20. Enthusiasm was high. "They were now once more in the face of the enemy," Salt reminded the council, "another day of moral strife was fast approaching, and every man must be found at his post."[32] The regional political unions again had to be enlisted. Although most of the approximately fifty unions in the district[33] apparently remained in existence, many had become virtually inactive. Still, the council managed to attract about thirty of them, and in addition to the previous participants the more distant unions located at Derby, Nottingham, Sheffield, and Tewkesbury agreed to attend. As an outside attraction, O'Connell was invited to speak. Attwood issued a personal appeal to the men of the Midlands to meet him at the old and hallowed site in order to lay their grievances at the foot of the throne; if they did so, he promised, "Our good King will again listen . . . The unjust Ministers will be dismissed; *and the Prosperity of the People will yet be restored.*"[34] More mundane tasks to be performed were the construction of a platform at the site, the employment of fifty constables to keep the peace, and the replacement of the many banners that bore slogans lauding the Whig ministers.

The weather on the 20th was favorable, and all accounts confirmed that the spectacle was, as Attwood had predicted, "a grand & beautiful sight."[35] The council had produced new flags and banners in profusion, and the trades lent their own bands and banners to the occasion. The national colors floated from several tall poles along the hill, and a huge blue banner with various inscriptions hung above the elaborate hustings erected at the foot of the slope. Everywhere on the perimeter of the area there were the booths and carts of vendors offering food and drink—one observer counted fifty-three ale booths on the field by 9 A.M. The grand procession this time included an open carriage, in which rode the two honored guests, Attwood and O'Connell, hailed as the liberators of England and Ireland. The deputations from other unions were escorted and cheered as before. With regard to attendance, the estimates varied enormously, the Tories citing computations as low as 20,000 persons, the reporters from *The Times* holding that perhaps 80,000 were present, and the unionists suggesting that the figure may have reached 230,000. The truth cannot be known, but the last estimate must have been far too high, since fewer and smaller deputations came to this meeting from the surrounding districts, and the council themselves complained that many employers within Birmingham had not freed the workers to attend. It likely was no oversight that the speakers this time did not refer to numbers. In addition, most observers noted that the holiday spirit and the presence of women and children were even more conspicuous than on previous occasions.

The speeches were infused with strong royalist sentiments. Muntz proclaimed that the throne was their last resource, and Attwood said that William was not to blame for their afflictions—bad councilors beset him. As for the question of who might replace the present ministers, Attwood stated that only the king was the proper judge of that. The banker also summed up the intent of the meeting: "We set today a great example in the Midland districts. If that example should be followed up, as I trust it will be by our fellow-countrymen generally, we shall succeed in overturning this ministry quite as easily as we succeeded in placing them in power."[36]

In contrast to their confidence publicly expressed during the meeting, the council admittedly were depressed during the following days as they awaited results and assessed the event. The feeling that the affair somehow had misfired was heightened by the scornful reaction of the press. On the morning after the meeting *The Times* carried a belittling description written by its own reporters, and in the following issues it termed the whole thing "a good and merry fair." The *Morning Chronicle* printed a long excerpt from this account rather than from the *Proceedings,* as did most of the provincial press. Examples of the latter's reaction were the remarks of the *Manchester Guardian,* which charged that the unionists were disgruntled solely because the government would not accept their scheme for "cheating all the creditors in the kingdom," and the action of the *Leeds Mercury,* which gave the Birmingham story one paragraph's notice behind a four-column report of a local antislavery meeting.[37] Only Cobbett and a few other radicals seemed to take the enterprise seriously. In the council's sessions there was much despondent talk of what to do if the petition failed. Several councilmen advised a nonpayment of taxes, but others were doubtful about the tactic. Some of the Radicals talked of a campaign for universal suffrage: if the reformed Parliament persisted in backing a wicked administration, they pointed out, then democracy was necessary to change the government. But they too got no encouragement. Salt proposed that the council "assemble and consult with all the really patriotic members of Parliament," a piece of presumptuous advice that fell dead. Finally they decided to adjourn for a fortnight.[38]

The full reality of their position was acknowledged by the council when they reassembled. Only two or three meetings had been held in the country to support them, and any hope of finding funds to organize agitation elsewhere seemed dim in view of a recent failure to increase the income of the union by the use of voluntary collectors. All of the councilmen agreed that there was no unity of purpose among the middle- and lower-class reformers of the country and that no one now seemed prepared to follow the lead of Birmingham. Muntz concluded that the members of the union either had to pay their dues or see the organization dissolved.[39]

The union's annual meeting was postponed from July to September, and although Attwood returned home and urged upon his old associates increased energy and perseverance, the meeting when held generated little enthusiasm and was poorly attended.[40] Thereafter the council reportedly met only five times during the remainder of the year, a fact that prompted an opponent to sneer that not much deliberative wisdom was issuing these days from the "obscure attic in Great Charles-street."[41] Already the council had begun to disband the organization. In November they closed the reading room and reduced their paid staff to one clerk and one collector. In February 1834, they discharged the remaining employees and closed the office of the union, except for four evenings a week when one of the councilmen would be present for two hours "to receive all monies and transact the business of the Union."[42] A special meeting of all persons who had at any time sat on the council was summoned by circular to gather at a local hotel the same month, evidently in an effort to persuade them to share in the debt of the union.[43] There is no evidence of success. If the council convened and deliberated during the next several months, no one bothered to report it.

Finally, on June 3, 1834, the leaders of the union met and determined to suspend the society indefinitely. Their resolution stated that the "unhappy discords which have latterly broken out in many parts of the kingdom between the lower and middle classes of the people, render any combined operations for their mutual benefit extremely difficult or altogether impossible." A committee was appointed to give up the union's rooms and discharge its debts.[44] And so the union formally ceased to function, "having been preceded to the grave," a provincial editor observed, "by almost every Political Union in England."[45] Like most of the council's activities during the past two years, this final action attracted little attention.

CHAPTER VI

Transition to Democracy

July 1834–December 1837

THE REFORM BILL had restored hope, Attwood wrote at the end of 1834, and thus the union had "sunk to rest like an infant on its mother's breast."[1] It was a fitful repose, however, characteristic more of restless men than of infants. The leading councilmen especially were inclined to be restive. To men who had stood before thousands of followers at Newhall Hill, who had received cheers when they arrived at and spoke in their own chamber, and who had imagined that the Empire anxiously awaited their addresses, to such men it was unthinkable to return fully to metal rolling, buttonmaking, and lamp manufacturing—whatever the truth of the *Argus's* jeer that it was entirely for these tasks that both nature and education had prepared them. Nor were the members of the union content to forego permanently the excitement of participating in great political pageants and of being told that they were responsible for epochal reforms. The next three years, therefore, witnessed various attempts by some of the more zealous unionists to rouse the society from its torpor and to set it moving on a fresh campaign.

To stir the "slumbering giant" to action of any sort was not easy, for the times were placid. Almost everyone but Attwood and his immediate followers was prepared to admit that the mercantile and manufacturing sections of the economy were prosperous, if agriculture was not. The only groups still pressing for change on a national level were the trade unionists and the evangelicals, and they tended to rely mainly upon their own organizations and to pursue goals—wage agreements and temperance laws—which had little or no appeal to other agitators. In fact the abstemious Attwood himself incurred the wrath of the Birmingham temperance spokesmen about this time with a speech arguing the right of the poor man to get drunk; one of the crusaders retorted that they did not seek total abstinence, for a little drink might help exorcise Attwood's gloomy view of the monetary system.[2] It was a particularly effective gibe because the zeal and perseverance of the currency faction against hard money closely rivaled the feelings of the temperance forces against hard drink. At a dinner honoring the unionist Pierce for being an inactive churchwarden, for example, Salt characteristically warned that the farmers and manufacturers alike were in a "deplorable condition," and the following month he attempted unsuccessfully to form a new political association to seek an alteration in the currency.[3]

The political reality with which the ex-council now had to live was that they, along with the Radicals of the country, were not immune from the twists and turns of party politics after the passage of the reform bill. Although the bill did not divest the old landed and commercial oligarchy of its influence in the counties and older boroughs, it immediately altered the political situation in the newly enfranchised towns. Here the political factions for the first time found themselves unavoidably geared to elections, parliamentary alliances, and ministerial policies. For agitators of all stripes the Liberal party, although Whiggish and composed of tepid reformers at best, was in fact the only practical alternative to a Conservative, or Tory, government, and thus to agitate against the Grey and Melbourne ministries was in effect to work for the return of Wellington and Peel. In November 1834, the Radicals of England were abruptly confronted with this unhappy dilemma of party politics when the king dismissed the Liberal government and recalled the Conservatives to power. O'Connell spoke for most Radicals at this point when he declared that he would go on his knees to join any man in preventing the entrenchment of a Conservative government. The ex-council could not avoid the same bothersome choice, and the result was that they too were soon drawn into declaring support for the former ministers, an endorsement expressed in their case by a working alliance with the Birmingham Whigs and Dissenters.

The unlikely entente between the unionists and the Whigs and Dissenters (who now fashionably termed themselves Liberals) continued for two years and effectively repressed the crusading impulses of the ex-councilmen for the entire period. The alliance was not without friction and embarrassment on both sides, of course, and it was made more difficult still by Attwood's hostility to it. The banker proclaimed that a "terrible revolution" was imminent unless Peel's Act was abolished, and he did not fail to remind the unionists that the ministers they wanted reinstated were the same traitors for whose dismissal they had called the year before.[4] But his old associates deserted him and the alliance continued even after the Liberal government was restored to power.

The partnership was a complicated juncture of the four different factions making up the two groups before the passage of the reform bill. The unionist Radicals and the Dissenters found common ground in their support of reformist issues, particularly in their opposition to the Established Church (which duly condemned them as the "combined forces of Infidelity and Dissent") and their support of factory and antislavery legislation. They held meetings and successfully compelled Attwood and Scholefield to take a stand on the antislavery issue, and to express general support of their other causes. The Ultra-Tories and the Whigs, on the other hand, were lukewarm on the matter of most reforms, and they found common cause principally in their opposition to the Conservatives, who were growing more assertive locally and who had established political contacts with the Tory gentry nearby. The Ultra-Tories on occasion deserted the Whigs and joined the trades' spokesmen in town in an "England first" opposition to antislavery and Irish measures, but the Whigs made more compatible allies. In practice Scholefield sloughed off his former unionist sentiments and served as the Whig representative, while Attwood continued to represent the Ultra-Tory unionists. Attwood found the restraints of party politics far more galling than did Scholefield, and he talked repeatedly of resigning as M.P., but to the disappointment of the Liberals he consistently changed his mind.

Ironically, it was the ex-council's hesitant consorting with the

Liberals which led to a partial revival of the union. On August 18, 1835, the council joined with the Liberals in sponsoring a public meeting to petition the House of Lords for passage of the municipal corporation bill introduced by the Melbourne government.[5] Although two previous attempts to reestablish the union had proved abortive, some of the former leaders saw in the new confrontation with the Lords an excellent opportunity to restore the union to life. Why not reactivate the society for the express purpose of carrying municipal reform just as they had won parliamentary reform? They would once more side with the ministers, and they could work with other reformers, both locally and nationally, for this single object. The idea was appealing, and in September a part of the ex-council arranged a public meeting which proclaimed the union alive and well.[6]

But bad luck still plagued the unionists. Hardly had they reestablished the union when the government compromised with the Lords on the municipal reform bill and both Houses passed the amended version. The revived organization was left with no major issue to agitate, and the best that it could do was to join the Liberals in political jousting with the local Conservatives, competition centering on public dinners and voter registration and in which the council and their Liberal allies were generally outeaten and outregistered. In the summer of 1836, therefore, the councilmen decided to transform the moribund society into an organization more in keeping with the times and the party politics in which they in fact had come to engage. The reconstituted organization sought Liberals as participants and was given the title of "The Birmingham and Midland Reform Association"; Philip Henry Muntz, younger brother of George Frederick and an equally large and bearded but less volatile man, became chairman. Even Attwood now came about and approved of the changes in identity and role of the society. The times were prosperous and so there was no need for agitation, he said, but the boroughmongers yet possessed great power and it was by no means improbable that they would make another attempt to plunder the people; in the meantime it was necessary to conserve the union's moral power until the occasion when it would be needed.[7]

Despite pronouncements to the contrary, the alliance between the former political enemies in Birmingham was wearing thin by 1837. The Dissenters, who composed about two-thirds of the Liberal party, were unhappy that Attwood and Scholefield retained both of Birmingham's seats in Parliament, thereby excluding a Dissenter from the honor. The Dissenters also quarreled increasingly with the Radicals over religious questions such as temperance, and at length they founded their own newspaper *(The Reformer)* and drew up their own list of candidates for local offices.[8] The Ultra-Tories meanwhile grumbled that not a single Whig had joined the Reform Association, and both they and the Whigs began to absent themselves from each other's meetings. More serious, the Whigs used their contacts with the Melbourne ministry to garner almost all of the patronage in Birmingham to the Liberals, leaving the unionists with party power but not the fruits of it. Some new alignment of the factions clearly was in the offing.

By now the council had had three years in which to reflect upon the past achievements and failures of the union. Among these leaders of the society the old myth refused to die. The passage of time merely strengthened their belief that almost alone they somehow had originated, directed, and sustained the movement for parliamentary reform. This being true, there was no room for questioning the basic formula of the union—that is, the use of the moral strength of the people by a few self-appointed leaders. If things had gone awry in 1833, it was a failure of application, of tactics, rather than of principle. And yet, how to prevent a repetition of the humiliation of 1833? By 1836 Attwood had decided that new methods were needed, with the council this time going to the people personally instead of relying upon the press or upon other societies to convey their moralist manifestoes. Also, he talked now of action only in behalf of the "working classes" or of the "mass of the people," not of a union of the middle and lower classes. If the oligarchs should again "put the *screw* upon the workmen," the banker declared,

. . . then I will tell you how to proceed. [*Loud cheering.*] You must raise five thousand pounds in the first place. You must then send delegations throughout the kingdom, to call meetings of the people in a hundred districts. [*Cheers.*] You must explain to them their own and their country's wrongs, and you must offer to lead them, and to guide them legally and peacefully into the measures necessary for their redress . . . . They will assemble on the first day of every month, to the number of two millions of men, and, in a voice of thunder, they will re-echo from a thousand centres the cordial and efficient support of any measure which the Birmingham Union may recommend. [*Cheers.*] In this way, my friends, you may be enabled to carry any measure you please, that is just, righteous, and beneficial. . . .[9]

Such changes obviously went beyond the realm of tactics. The old Birmingham unionist myth was being altered, adapted to a new situation, and in the process it was being separated from the local beliefs that had spawned and nurtured it. Being abandoned now was the idea that an ancient unity of classes alone could sanction political agitation. Gone even was the belief that such a harmony was possible. Also being discarded was the idea that Birmingham was a chosen city that by itself could lead the nation in the paths of political righteousness. As late as 1833 Attwood had boasted that "I have never attended a political meeting out of my native town, and it is not my intention ever to do so, unless extreme circumstances should require it."[10] The new talk was of the necessity of personal contact with and direction of people outside of Birmingham. And further changes in position were yet to come: the difficulty with Attwood's proposed scheme was that he still did not recognize the need for close cooperation with leaders elsewhere in the nation, or the necessity of adopting the democratic goals which the radicals would demand as the price of their cooperation.

Hard times gradually returned to Britain in 1837. Like prophets of doom whose deepest fear is that their worst predictions will fail, the council seemed almost relieved and inspired by the distress. At the first sign of the downturn in trade, they reminded everybody that they had forewarned the nation and that they had been ignored. Now they would be heeded, for, as Salt wrote in a letter to the *Journal*, "Distress, Mr. Editor, is coming, 'like a destroying Angel': no time is to be lost."[11] When the recession reached across the Atlantic to America, Attwood, who interpreted the American Revolution and subsequent history as a struggle for paper currency, wrote triumphantly, "I am happy to say that there is still a just God in heaven, & that Gen[era]l Jackson is ruined by his own measures, combined with those of Sir Robert Peel."[12] At least the course of the council now seemed clear: they must at once reconvert the reform association into the political union, the only body capable of handling great national crises.

The leaders of the reform association gathered at a special meeting on April 18 to plan the revival of the union. The speakers all agreed that the transformation should occur; the only problem was whether they could secure adequate finances. A possible solution appeared when editor Robert Douglas of the *Journal*, a shrewd Scotchman, suggested that they issue quarterly membership tickets at 6d. each and thus require members to pay upon entry into the society. Since the dues would amount to only half the subscription demanded by the old union, he calculated that a minimum of 4,000 men, or one-tenth of the working force of Birmingham, should readily respond. The *Journal* office could issue the tickets, removing the need for a staff and collectors, and ensuring that the £100 or more gathered each quarter would be clear income. The plan was attractive, and the meeting enthusiastically resolved that as soon as 4,000 men purchased tickets of membership the council would revive the "talismanic name of the Political Union." Then, Pierce said, the council must declare to the rulers of the country that they would not permit them to remain in power one hour unless there was action to relieve the distress.

A month later, on May 23, 1837, the metamorphosis of the society officially took place.[13] It was a significant event in Birmingham, for, however exaggerated was the council's claim that the union once had terrified all the tyrants of Europe, there was no doubt that locally it had been powerful and that its reappearance stirred strong emotions. The Conservatives launched an intensive attack upon the revived society, distributing leaflets charging the council with craftily restoring a fat goose for their personal profit, and advertising a declaration against the union signed by hundreds of business and professional men. The council, hypersensitive as ever to criticism, answered the attack by publishing a cheap pamphlet edition of the names of the signers of the declaration and calling upon the members of the union not to trade with them.[14]

The next step in the restoration of the union was a ceremony to reinstall the council in office. A gathering of the members, who soon numbered over 5,000, was held at the town hall on June 7. The big question until the last moment was whether Attwood would lend his name to the fresh endeavor. The former chairman increasingly had withdrawn from active contact with his Birmingham colleagues and had become convinced that the currency crisis was at hand and that he might be called into high office to put right the disjointed times. In fact, only a few days before the decision to resurrect the union Attwood wrote his wife that "I shall be very careful in committing myself."[15] The situation suddenly changed, however, when on June 5, two days prior to the election of the council, the banker suffered still another defeat in the House of Commons on a motion to alter the currency. The first sentence of his three-hour speech—"The House of Commons appeared to him to be like Nero fiddling whilst Rome was burning"—raised a snigger, and much of the rest encountered interjections and noisy laughter, with great hilarity on both sides of the House greeting his statement that "he did not like to spread anything like alarm." A mere twenty-three M.P.s voted with him.[16] The next morning Attwood wrote his former associates at Birmingham that he would never desert them, and they responded by making him president of the restored union.[17]

Of the thirty-four men elected to the council on June 7, only fifteen had served on the ruling body of the former union— Attwood, G. F. Muntz, Hadley, Edmonds, Salt, Felix Luckcock, and John Winfield, all of whom were charter members, plus Trow, Giles, Pierce, Jennings, Boultbee, and three others who subsequently had come to the council table. Later the aging and ailing Emes was also restored to their midst. Gone were such former leaders as Charles Jones, who had experienced financial difficulties, eventually losing his medalist business and turning to gun manufacturing, and who now seldom participated in political meetings; Pare, who had served the Liberals sufficiently well as a registration agent to be rewarded with a governmental appointment as superintendent registrar of marriages and deaths and who already had withdrawn from unionist activities in anticipation of it; and Bosco Attwood, who accepted a post in a new bank and "retired" from public affairs, fulfilling a statement made earlier to his brother that he was heartily sick of politics and planned to "cut his stick."[18] Dead by this time were Biddle and several other councilmen, and ill and destined to die within a few months was Urban Luckcock. Also, a principal leader whose name did reappear on the council list would not be active: G. F. Muntz was made vice-president of the union along with his brother Philip Henry, but for many months he had participated only slightly in local politics and now he was preparing to move to Wales to be near the operations of the chief producers of his patented "Muntz metal."

Two of the nineteen newcomers to the council were to be ranked with Attwood, Salt, and Edmonds as the body's most influential spokesmen. The better known of the two was P. H. Muntz, formerly chairman of the reform association and now in the absence of his brother the person who was to preside over most of the meetings of the council of the union. A merchant by trade, he also increasingly looked after his brother's metal-rolling mill in Birmingham; by this time he had a reputation, in the words of a colleague, of being "notoriously the very best attender and the hardest worker in all matters of public business in town." The other tyro, Robert K. Douglas, likewise had made his mark in the reform association. A tall man with a fine shock of prematurely grey hair, Douglas had both the commanding appearance and the oratorical ability of a leader. Although only in his early forties, he had changed party loyalties several times, having been in turn a Whig, a Tory, and now a "Tory Radical." As the new editor of the *Journal* he was in a position to further the union by giving it free publicity and by lending the use of his office and staff in performing his duties as treasurer of the society. His colleagues accordingly applauded his services even when he reported his own speeches to the near exclusion of theirs.

The most prominent of the other novice councilmen were Charles Sturge, corn factor and member of a leading Dissenter

family, and William Scholefield, son of the former deputy-chair-
man, but both immediately became inactive. The rest were generally men of small means and, the opponents of the union
claimed, men also of small ability. Most of them apparently were
supporters of Attwood's currency views. They included nine
manufacturers of various items, three merchants, and four professional men. Only Joseph Holl, a japanner who later was to
serve as secretary, and Isaac Aaron, a surgeon and the only Jew
on the council, were to participate significantly in the business of
the union. There were no workingmen on the governing body and
no provisions for consultation with the membership of the union,
evidence that the aristocratic propensities of the founders
remained unchanged, despite the almost exclusive working-class
enrollment of the society.[19]

With this election of the council the reorganization of the union
was completed. But what of a program? It soon developed that,
for the moment at least, the union was to operate entirely upon
its founders' original set of principles and policies, without resort
even to enlarged tactics of the kind advocated by Attwood the
year before. The hallowed legend of the early years persisted too
strongly to be displaced easily, especially amid the excitement of
a fresh campaign and with the addition of so many councilmen
who had not experienced the disillusionment of the demise of the
first union. Consequently the directors of the society largely
picked up where they had left off in 1834. In a special session
following their election they agreed to summon the inhabitants of
Birmingham to Newhall Hill to provide support for a deputation
to be sent to Lord Melbourne. The deputation would demand on
behalf of the British people three measures to restore happiness
and prosperity to the realm: repeal of Peel's Act of 1819; repeal
of the corn laws; and restoration of "ancient and constitutional
rights," consisting of household suffrage, shorter parliaments,
ballot, payment of M.P.s, and abolition of the property qualification. Later the council added a demand for repeal of the Poor
Law of 1834, perhaps because of the agitation on the subject then
developing in the North. The council anticipated that the tidings
of the union's again taking the field would arouse the nation

instantly to echo Birmingham's challenge to the government. Salt assured his colleagues that they were truly launching their second great moral campaign and that "the moment the banner of the old Union was unfurled—[Cheers]—the people would rally round it from all parts." Boultbee agreed, "the eyes of England were turned towards Birmingham, and awaiting their movements."[20]

Attendance at the Newhall Hill meeting on June 19, 1837, was estimated variously at 15,000 to 150,000 persons, depending on the prejudices of the observer. Since new buildings had narrowed the open space on the hill by one-third, there was a reduced upper limit placed upon the estimates. All of the old devices to generate excitement were employed, plus a "spirit-stirring address" from Attwood calling upon the people to meet him at the hallowed site in the previous manner. No appeal was needed, of course, to attract the ubiquitous dispensers of food and drink who always were present on such occasions, nor the many spectators who always came for the purpose of enjoying the sellers' wares. Overall, the affair perhaps did not come up quite to the standards of the early 1830s, but even the opposition admitted that it was not a total failure.

During the meeting several of the leaders dropped new hints of enlarged tactics if the society was ignored as it had been in 1833. Attwood, for example, repeated his threat to produce two million men banded together in a "sacred and solemn compact" and holding simultaneous meetings throughout the country in support of the union, and then he went on to add that if this tactic were ignored there might be a general strike of both masters and men for an entire week, a "sublime" spectacle such as "the wide earth and the wide range of history never exhibited before." A different recommendation came from Pierce, who enlarged upon a suggestion made earlier by Salt that the people send delegates to London from throughout the country to present their demands—let the people send 300,000 such delegates, he suggested.[21] The obvious problem with such talk was that the leaders of the union still assumed that the working classes of the country would enthusiastically endorse the program of moderate political change advocated by the union and that the council required no direct assistance from other reformers in marshaling millions of men. A month later, for example, the council all but ignored a request from the London Working Men's Association asking for their cooperation in seeking universal suffrage.[22]

The meeting appointed P. H. Muntz, Salt, and Hadley a deputation to confront Melbourne with the union's demands. Before the three agents could act, however, events elsewhere intervened. On the day following the meeting the king died. Custom dictated that a parliamentary election be held, and soon the country gave its attention to the speeches of candidates and not to the words of the council. Despite the distraction, the deputation, with Douglas substituting for Hadley, did see Melbourne on June 27, and they demanded extraordinary action by the government to free the nation from the tyranny of Peel's Act and from the other grievances of which they complained—if necessary, they urged, let the cabinet resort to illegal orders in council to accomplish the changes. The deputation reported back to the union their belief that Melbourne had been impressed by their words.[23] The country nevertheless paid no attention whatever to them, and the council themselves soon turned to the local reelection of Attwood and Scholefield as a primary concern. It was August before they could return to their campaign to save the nation.

The problem not yet solved was how to get the country to rally behind the council, or, indeed, even to be made aware of the union's existence. Some of the councilmen suggested that the union now must adopt Attwood's scheme for dispatching agitators to other places to rouse the people directly, but other speakers argued that they could not afford it. Once the excitement produced by the restoration of the union had abated, the number of subscribing members had dropped rapidly from 8,800 to about 3,000, reducing the quarterly income of the society to approximately £75, a fraction of the £5,000 Attwood had estimated they would need.[24] This handicap of a declining income seemed decisive, and for three months the council did nothing. Then in October they sent yet another deputation to Melbourne to request an inquiry into the state of the currency. The Radicals on the council by this time were thoroughly disgusted over the inactivity, but Attwood and Salt participated in the interview with Melbourne and preferred to wait a few more weeks to see if the government would act. Attwood's hopes were high: it was true that Parliament would do nothing, he wrote, for the M.P.s were "as ignorant as asses & as obstinate as hogs"; but the ministers were different, and had, "as I told them, no safety but to *jump into our Birm^m Boat*." When the Speech from the Throne to the new Parliament appeared a fortnight later, however, it not only failed to refer to the currency, it also did not mention the distress. "I always told you," Attwood gloomily reminded his wife, "that this was a *doomed* & a *God abandoned Land*."[25]

What should they do now? The old Ultra-Tory instinct was to seek refuge in the crown. Attwood shortly before had told Joseph Parkes that cabinet government was a "modern innovation" and that there should be a return to a system of sworn privy councilors, prompting the lawyer to remark that "Tom Attwood is as mad as a March hare." As recently as June, Salt too had talked of appealing to the throne.[26] But this time the union's leaders were inhibited in their royalist sentiments, for it was generally conceded that the new monarch, Victoria, was entirely under Melbourne's influence. There clearly was no choice but to look to the country and, since the Liberal and Conservative press persisted in ignoring the union, to find some means of approaching the people through agitators.

Furthermore, it became obvious at last to the entire council that a moderate program of political change would not attract the attention and support that the union wanted. Even Attwood finally was prepared to do what had to be done. In October, before returning to his parliamentary duties, the banker told the council that if the latest mission to Melbourne failed they must raise the standard of universal suffrage.

> When they could get two millions of men to move like clock work at the command of the union in a legal and constitutional manner, then indeed might they hope for success. But in order to effect this great and mighty union, they must go for a great measure of reform. [Hear, hear.] They must go for universal suffrage, because although he did not believe it could be proved to be a constitutional right, as household suffrage unquestionably was, yet it was a natural right, and one on which the great mass of the people had set their hearts, and for which they would contend.

A like view was expressed by P. H. Muntz, the presiding officer of the council after Attwood's departure, and other moderates such as Hadley, Salt, and Douglas soon indicated their concurrence.[27] The old Radicals on the council were delighted at this long-delayed conversion to democracy by the Tory Radicals, and they scarcely concealed their pleasure when the government failed to act on the currency issue. The outcome was that the council in December addressed the nation and proclaimed an intention to seek universal suffrage "as a rightful inheritance."[28]

Two further steps were needed to make the council's decision effective. One was a willingness to put aside the issue of the currency and to concentrate entirely upon demands for a change in the parliamentary representation. This action the council now resolved to take, it being obvious, as P. H. Muntz and Douglas argued, that people outside of Birmingham had no interest in the monetary question and would never support a campaign that included it. In December, Attwood returned from London and pleaded with his colleagues not to forsake wholly their old cause, but he lost out.[29] By this time the banker's closest followers had concluded, in the words of one disciple, that their leader was a century ahead of other men on the subject of the currency and therefore his ideas must await a future generation, much as the concepts of Galileo and other pioneers of truth had had to await the advent of more receptive minds.

The other step taken by the council was perhaps the most difficult of all. The chieftains of the union at last accepted that they, acting alone, could not agitate the country and therefore that they must seek the direct assistance of radical leaders in other towns. To this end Hadley on November 28, 1837, moved "with fear and trembling" that "the necessary steps be immediately taken to procure the co-operation of the Radical Reformers of England, Scotland, and Ireland" in a program of agitation. A week later, in announcing the union's espousal of democracy, the council advertised, *"The Men of Birmingham* will either lead or follow. Our name and our achievements might well entitle us to claim the van; but we shall cheerfully take our station wherever we can render most efficient service."[30]

The old local myth thus was further modified. The council were prepared to advocate, not ancient principles belonging to the people as matter of historical right, but rather the claims of a

123

single class, supported as a matter of political expediency. Also, the unionists finally seemed to realize that they must share leadership with men outside of Birmingham, to act directly with radicals who did not share the council's own outlook. For moralist knights of the old reform bill days it must have seemed a bastard mythology. Yet there was no preventing it, for times and illusions had changed.

The union's new departure in politics was confirmed in almost symbolic fashion in mid-December. On the 11th, the London Working Men's Association adopted a resolution applauding the conversion of the union to democracy, and the following day Henry Hetherington visited the council on the part of the association. The two groups exchanged assurances of mutual confidence.[31] Two days later O'Connell came to town. In a speech at the town hall, the "spiritual brother" of the Birmingham leaders defended the Liberal government and challenged the idea that the union had the power to make and unmake ministries. Muntz and Salt led an attack on him, and he left on the next train bitterly estranged from his former admirers.[32] The direction of the council now irreversibly was toward the movement for political democracy that later would be known as Chartism, and into that national movement they were to carry most of the apparent sources of strength and most of the grave weaknesses exhibited previously on a regional scale by the Birmingham union.

CHAPTER VII

The Union and the Development
of the Chartist Movement

January-July 1838

THE LEADERS OF THE UNION had taken their democratic vows and had pledged themselves to organize a great moral drive for universal manhood suffrage. Even so, a desire for secondary or private goals sometimes moves crusaders more powerfully to take the field than does a proclaimed objective, and so it was with the council of the union. The principal leaders of the society were aristocratic-minded Ultra-Tories who had dropped their objections to universal suffrage merely because monetary changes seemed unobtainable without mass agitation against the government and legislature, and because democracy seemed to be the only issue likely to stir the masses. The reservation they entertained about democracy is the key to understanding many of their actions in the coming Chartist campaign, for hesitant warriors are not likely to persist under adversity and inevitably they quarrel with fellow crusaders who question their loyalty and leadership.

Yet it was the council that proclaimed the fresh campaign, fixed its basic character, and developed its major tactics. The democracy they advocated was not to their own taste, but the movement for it bore their peculiar political stamp. Still fundamental to the council's thinking was the concept of politics as a moral confrontation between an uncorrupted people and evil conspirators, a struggle the people could always win if properly led. Attwood succinctly stated this doctrine when he said, "We have always acted upon the principle that the public opinion is omnipotent, and that it is only necessary to exhibit the public mind, combined and united, and acting simultaneously with one head, one heart, and one hand, to insure instant success in every just and righteous cause."[1] The council accordingly organized the new movement in this light, that is, expressly as a moral encounter, and however unrealistic their judgments and expectations may have been, the strategy they developed was merely an expanded version of what they believed had worked flawlessly in 1832.

Attwood's term, "exhibit the public mind," perhaps best defined the council's principal task. But how to proceed in doing this? Two problems had to be solved before the union's political and economic enemies could be engaged and defeated. (1) Contact had to be established with the radical reformers of the country. The council had shown a willingness to ally with the radicals in seeking universal suffrage, but how, specifically, was this cooperation to be arranged? (2) A plan of agitation had to be developed. The council had announced a willingness to work for radical political goals exclusively, but upon what plan was the movement to be conducted? The "voice of the people" had to be organized more efficiently than it had been in 1833-1834 if it was to arouse terror in the heart of anyone. The council gradually conceived answers to these problems, and, although from the beginning the effectiveness of their schemes was questionable, the basic tactics they developed were to be pursued by radical reformers throughout the early Chartist years.

The project first devised by the council soon failed. It was natural that the unionists in their talk of originating and directing simultaneous meetings of nearly half of the men in Britain should revive their old vision of commanding countless political unions and through them of confronting the oligarchs with a rival, more moral, authority. The scheme had the advantage of placing themselves at the center of things, for despite their proclamation offering either to lead or to follow it was not seriously supposed at Birmingham that the generals of 1832 should now become privates. The formation of unions would have to be started anew, of course, since the Birmingham union and one or two satellite societies were the only survivors of the agitation of the early thirties, and local reformers elsewhere would have to be enlisted in the endeavor. A committee of the council drafted a circular to one or more reformers in eight large towns (apparently mostly middle-class persons) and invited them to make such preparations as might assist a deputation to be sent from Birmingham to found unions in those places. The committee admitted that it was uncertain about whom to write, and also that the funds to enable the deputation to visit all of the places listed were not yet available, but it hoped the recipients of the circular would respond enthusiastically and that the members of the Birmingham union would contribute adequate money once the campaign developed. Attwood predicted that by May Day the council would have two million men banded together in an invincible organization which "would govern any government that ever existed."[2]

The project completely misfired. To be sure, the members of the union met on January 15 and dutifully voted permission for the council to choose a deputation to go forth in the name of the union. Both Attwood and G. F. Muntz put in an appearance to give the occasion *éclat*, and a majority of the 3,000 members attended. The major problem was that the reformers to whom the council's circular had been sent either refused to assist in the campaign or took no notice of it at all, and thus they left the Birmingham leaders with no committed supporters around whom unions elsewhere could be organized and directed.[3] The sole definite invitation received by the council was from Coventry, a town that was not on the committee's list, and, although several councilmen hurried there and made speeches at a rally much more radical than what they were accustomed to deliver at home,[4] the event proved to be the concluding rather than the opening gun of the drive to organize the country around Birmingham by means of unions.

In truth, political unions of the Birmingham variety—that is, professed combinations of the middle and lower classes—had become political anachronisms. As the council themselves soon admitted, the middle classes in 1838, depressed or not, were unwilling to unite with the workers in a demand for further constitutional changes. In Birmingham even the shopkeeper class shunned the cause, the only exception being about two-thirds of the publicans, in whose houses the "sections" of the union had gathered. The council's appeal to the workers in fact produced a

new political front in Birmingham, a coalition between the unionists and the leaders of the trades' societies, organizations of
skilled laborers which had 13,000 members in the city and which
had survived the earlier breakup of the national labor unionist
movement. The trades individually had lent their bands and banners to the political union's rallies in the reform bill agitation, but
no formal ties existed between them and the council. The chief
spokesmen for these societies at present were four workingmen,
Henry Watson, Thomas Baker, Joseph Corbett, and Samuel
Brown. These men had been largely nonpolitical in their activities until now, although they were staunch democrats and had
cooperated with Hunt and Wade in the founding of a short-lived
working-class political union in Birmingham late in 1832.[5] After
the council's espousal of democracy they came forward to offer
their support.[6] The council willingly accepted the offer, but the
working-class leaders for the moment were treated as supporters
rather than as equals, persons who were permitted to bring written declarations to the council but who were not given seats on
that body. Yet as some of the Radicals later grew wary of the
movement and became inactive, the influence of these new political spokesmen for the workers, as well as that of other, more
violent workingmen, inevitably was to increase. In Birmingham
the old grandee form of the "union of the industrious classes"
was dead, never to be resurrected.

What was true of Birmingham was even more so for the rest of
the nation: when a few, scattered political unions finally did
appear in the country, they were mostly radical ones of the working classes with little or no middle-class membership. Like the
Huntite societies before them, they were deeply suspicious of the
Birmingham union, and later they were to be among its severest
critics. Yet it was not even unions of this stripe that were to be
the main source of agitation in the new movement; rather, it was
working men's associations, societies which like the radical
unions sought mainly lower-class support and which grew rapidly
in 1837 and 1838. Most of the working men's associations were
modeled on the London organization founded in 1836 under the
leadership of William Lovett, Henry Hetherington, John Cleave,
and James Watson, with Lovett as secretary and leading spirit.
Although rather high dues in the beginning kept enrollment lim-

ited generally to skilled workmen, and they were committed to educational and parliamentary tactics rather than to mass agitation, in title and origin they were more logically the sponsors of a democratic movement than were the political unions. By the spring of 1838 there were reportedly about 150 of the associations in the country.[7] An example of their appeal was the Birmingham leaders' difficulty in persuading the reformers at Coventry to reestablish a union there instead of founding an association.

It seems possible that the working men's associations might have continued to increase greatly in number and influence and have totally eclipsed the Birmingham union, but early in 1838 a rancorous quarrel broke out between the founders of the parent London society and a group of radicals aligned with Feargus O'Connor, an aggressive Irishman and publisher of the *Northern Star* at Leeds, who was emerging as the leading radical agitator in the North. O'Connor's followers began to establish rival "democratic associations" which advocated more aggressive tactics and a broader program of change, including repeal of the Poor Law. Many working men's associations, particularly in the North, began to ally with them rather than with Lovett's moderate society. Hence from the start the organizations destined to conduct the new agitation were divided and suspicious of each other. The Birmingham Political Union and the London Working Men's Association at this point occupied a common moderate ground in comparison to the position of the O'Connorite radicals, yet cooperation between them was to be difficult because each regarded itself as the natural leader of any national campaign. After the initial address of the L.W.M.A. welcoming the Birmingham union to the democratic fold the two societies had little contact as each pursued its own policies and apparently hoped that the other would assume a subordinate position.

The council, of course, were now faced with the task of devising fresh tactics to replace the defunct scheme for agitation through political unions. At a session in February Salt declared that the union must press on immediately with some new plan, before the deepening quicksand swallowed them all. He recommended that they dispatch a delegation to Glasgow, where he believed the distress had made the people unusually receptive to agitation.

> From this northern point they would proceed southward, gathering strength as they went, and rolling forward a great moral avalanche . . . From every town as they went on in their holy and peaceful pilgrimage, they would send one and the same petition, sanctioned by great public meetings, and claiming the whole of the rights of the people. . . . Having thus concentrated and given unity to the efforts of the people, and the will of the nation having been unequivocally declared, and their universal petition laid before Parliament, he then proposed to hold, throughout England, a day of solemn observance, in which all the people should meet and enter into a covenant to abstain from all taxed and exciseable articles, from spirits, beer, sugar, teas, &c., until their full and just rights were restored.

The council reacted favorably to this plan, and they began to talk of obtaining from one to six million signatures to the document, which was soon termed a "national petition."[8] Further reflection upon the cost and labor of the enterprise, however, led them to revise their own role to that of staging a giant meeting in Glasgow and possibly one or two other places and then depending upon these examples to excite radical reformers elsewhere to take similar action. The initial momentum, in other words, would be the union's contribution to the movement, and all the rest somehow would follow, just as it had in 1830.

The idea of a national petition had a number of precedents, including the council's own proposal for a national "Solemn Declaration" against Wellington in 1832. But if the proposal was not entirely new, it does seem clear that the council acted alone in making it the basis of a movement for democracy. Most radicals avowedly were disillusioned with the practice of petitioning an unresponsive legislature, and until revived on an enormous scale by the union the tactic was held in considerable disrepute among them. The O'Connorites later agreed to the maneuver only as "one final effort" at petitioning, and the L.W.M.A. from the start was highly critical of the proposal. The association in fact had its own plan, the product of a meeting in June 1837, which had appointed a committee of six members of the association and six radical M.P.s to draft a parliamentary bill embodying six points—universal manhood suffrage, annual parliaments, the ballot, equal electoral districts, and no property qualification for and payment of M.P.s. Lovett and his associates intended for this bill, called the "People's Charter," to become the object of a lengthy, peaceful campaign conducted by the working men's associations in the country. As late as December 1837, however, the committee appointed to draw up the bill had not met, and at the end of the following March, over a month after Salt had proposed a national petition to the council of the Birmingham union, Lovett still was trying to get the committee to finish its work.[9]

Although a step behind the union in devising agitation, the L.W.M.A. and other associations nevertheless did influence the council to enlarge their objectives. When the union's conversion to democracy was announced in December 1837, the Birmingham leaders had limited their demands to universal manhood suffrage, the ballot, and "frequent parliaments." It was a regressive decision on their part, for there had been prior talk of other points by individual councilmen. Immediately the L.W.M.A. and the Bath and Leeds associations in replying to the union's address called attention to its omission of other radical goals, and the L.W.M.A. particularly stressed the need for abolishing the property qualification.[10] The result was that when Salt recommended the tactic of a national petition two months later he and the council included repeal of the property qualification and payment of M.P.s, leaving off only the demand for equal electoral districts (on the ground that it was "not in accord with ancient custom"). In return for this enlargement of the union's goals, Lovett's group seemed to have acquiesced tacitly in the council's refusal to endorse annual parliaments, for in its address to the union the association spoke now of "short parliaments," a euphemism for triennial ones.

The council's adoption of Salt's plan for agitation in behalf of a national petition meant that one of the requirements for a new campaign had been met. The second prerequisite, that of finding some acceptable method of cooperating with the radicals of the country, was now dealt with also. In the following session of the council, P. H. Muntz declared that there must be some authoritative body to direct the project of abstention from taxable commodities which was planned as the climax of the drive, and he proposed that all of the large towns in Britain elect special representatives to convene at a central place to oversee the agitation.[11] In recommending this scheme Muntz probably was influenced by a recent speech of O'Connell in which the Irish leader, although now a moderate supporter of the government, reminded his English audience that the law did not prohibit meetings of delegates in their own country as it did in Ireland.[12] The council eagerly accepted Muntz's proposal. Not only would an assembly of delegates provide the Birmingham leaders with a body to whose custody the national petition eventually could be entrusted, relieving the union of primary responsibility for the fate of that document, but it would facilitate eventual, direct contact with the radical chieftains of the country, relieving the council meanwhile of the necessity of immediate communication and deliberation with them. Gradually for the unionists the projected convention replaced the monarch as a kind of final authority, permitting the council to escape all of their political dilemmas by postponing them for the attention of the future "deputies of the people."

The new dogma on which the Birmingham union prepared to act was like the old one mainly in its belief in the efficacy of moral action. In all other respects it was a transplanted myth, without the peculiar ingredients which were combined in its earlier form. No longer was there talk of a harmonious unity of the people, of ancient rights sanctioned by history and the crown, and of a chosen center of agitation. Even the old apocalyptic and utopian strains now were muted, for the evil enemies of the people were even less identifiable than before, the prophecies of an armageddon clash with them were less prominent, and the proclamations of a coming age of prosperity and harmony were far less pronounced. The myth was being generalized, divorced from Birmingham, something perhaps best described as moral action based upon the myth of former moral action. Only in strategy did the new campaign retain the characteristics of the previous moral crusade; the unionists still avoided direct confrontation with their vague enemies, and also avoided direct, immediate contact with their outside friends. The major activity of the campaign was to consist of meetings and the gathering of signatures to a petition, to be followed by abstinence from taxable items. There would be no head-on conflict with the authorities, and the council's allies would be consulted in a future assembly after the principal agitation was over. Moral action thus remained indirect action from afar. Even the decision to go to Glasgow kept to this pattern, for the Scottish city in a sense was specially selected to represent the outside world for the unionists.

Not yet solved, of course, was the council's need for prompt communication with the radical reformers of Glasgow, where the union's leaders proposed to launch their crusade. Salt suggested as a solution that they dispatch to Glasgow an agent, "a sort of St. John, to prepare the way," who could locate potential allies there and arrange for a great meeting to receive the full delegation from Birmingham. John Collins, a newcomer to the council, warmly endorsed the idea and declared that the prophet sent to proclaim their coming must be a man of courage, enthusiasm, and prudence. Perhaps the journeyman penmaker's colleagues here sensed his willingness to undertake the assignment, a readiness enhanced by the fact that he almost alone on the council was not tied down with business or professional duties. In any case they soon appointed him and agreed to pay him for the work.[13]

During the interval in which Collins began his political labors in Scotland the council largely marked time. As in the past, inactivity widened the existing divisions among them, and these weeks of waiting were enlivened by several affrays reminiscent of earlier squabbles. Only Boultbee, however, resigned as a result. One local issue did draw them together: the movement to obtain a charter for the town, started when the Liberals and the unionists were political allies, now came before the Privy Council. Despite their fresh differences the proposers of incorporation joined in thwarting a belated effort by Conservatives to defeat the application. The Conservative faction feared that the leaders at the council table of the union would soon sit around the table of the town council, and in this it turned out that their fears were fully justified.

The most curious public event to occur in Birmingham during this period undoubtedly was the convening of a large political meeting of women. Salt was the guiding hand behind the move, for he believed that his abstinence plan would not work without the participation of women, who were the principal purchasers of tea. To get the support of those in Birmingham, he met with an estimated 12,000 females on April 2 in "such a sight as was never before beheld by mortal eye." Amid enthusiastic clapping of hands and waving of handkerchiefs he had them pledge obedience to the leaders of the union. Most of his colleagues on the council cowardly denied any connection with the enterprise because of the abundant ridicule heaped upon it by the observers of the day; but Salt remained undaunted and he soon expanded his master plan for agitation to include a call for meetings of women throughout Britain.[14]

Collins by this time had begun to send back optimistic reports on his reception in Scotland and on the prospects for agitation in that country. Although there was some truth to a Tory critic's sneer that no "paid itinerant demagogue" ever returned unfavorable reports, Collins did prove to be an exceptionally good choice for the assignment. He was a slightly built man of undistinguished appearance, yet he had a pleasant voice and an unaffected manner which quickly won the respect of the Scottish reformers. Above all, he was dedicated to his task as perhaps only one who is rising in political or social rank can be; later he declared that he attended an average of three meetings every day during his stay in Scotland.[15] By the second week in April he had enlisted the cooperation of the radical section of the old Glasgow Political Union, led principally by James Moir, James Turner, and Alexander Purdie. They in turn had won support from the trade unions and other working-class organizations of the city for a "grand demonstration" there on May 21 to inaugurate the council's national crusade.[16] Soon afterward Collins proceeded to Edinburgh and to several of the provincial towns in an effort to enlist working-class radical support for meetings to be held in those places as well.[17]

134

With the Glasgow inaugural of the great moral campaign now definitely set, the council had to draft their national petition and decide when and upon what basis deputies to the national convention should be selected. Addressing themselves to the latter problem first, the council suggested that reformers in each of the principal towns meet and choose one deputy for every 20,000 or so inhabitants. They then announced plans to hold a Newhall Hill meeting at Birmingham to approve the national petition and to appoint a group of men to serve both as delegates to the Glasgow meeting and, afterward, as Birmingham's deputies to the convention. A complication in the local plans developed, however, when Attwood suddenly intervened. The president of the union had been consulted only infrequently by the council after the movement had taken its new turn, and although he professed acceptance of his diminished role it is clear that he strongly resented it. His part in the entire Chartist episode of 1838–1839 in fact became an odd one from this point on. At heart he was even less a democrat than were most of his unionist colleagues, and so from the start he maintained a position of cool detachment toward the movement, yet he was unwilling to see the campaign proceed without his being placed at the head of it. This desire for the chief position later led him to claim personal credit, falsely, for almost the entire plan of agitation. On this occasion he wrote at the last minute and insisted that the meeting at Birmingham be delayed until after the delegation's return from the North, when the growing excitement, he said, would allow them to amass greater numbers. The council were annoyed and perplexed at the interference, but finally they agreed to hold only a preliminary meeting at the town hall on May 14 to appoint the delegation to Scotland and approve of a draft of the national petition, and then sometime later stage a great demonstration to appoint the deputies to the convention.

The drafting of the national petition was accomplished during this fortnight before the meeting on May 14 and it was done in a remarkably casual fashion for a document that was expected to change the course of British history. On May 1 the council appointed a committee, consisting of Salt, Edmonds, P. H. Muntz, Douglas, and three others, to make arrangements for the forthcoming town meeting, including the preparation of the petition. Douglas by now had succeeded Attwood as the principal drafter of the union's addresses and petitions and so the committee gave him the task of composing this one. The result was a document exhibiting the sententious and rhetorical style characteristic of the treasurer's hand. The content of the petition, however, could not be attributed to Douglas at all, for suddenly he had qualms about including anything more than universal suffrage and the ballot in the petition. Still, he argued in vain. The rest of the committee not only overrode his objections and kept all five points previously espoused by the council, but also they substituted annual for triennial parliaments, thus arriving finally at the full program favored by a majority of radical reformers. After it had completed its work the committee reported directly to the town meeting rather than back to the council.[18]

The reason for the committee's approval of annual parliaments was not stated, but the decisive pressure for it apparently came from Collins. On his trip through Lancashire and Scotland he had yielded to the sentiment of the Northerners on the question, and at this very time he was advocating the measure in Scotland as the agent of the union.[19] The consequence was that the leaders of the society had either to repudiate him or to adopt the goal themselves; the latter was the sensible plan, being a frank acknowledgment that the price of playing radical politics was a radical program.

At this point the question arises as to the relative credit to be assigned to the Birmingham union and to the London Working Men's Association for the formal commencement of the Chartist agitation. Historians have tended to date the beginning of the movement from the first public presentation of the documents containing the Chartist demands, and almost all writers have followed Place in assigning precedence in time to the Charter over the national petition. It is an erroneous judgment, for the two core documents of the Chartist movement were produced almost simultaneously, even though the basic program unquestionably derived from the L.W.M.A. and other radical groups rather than from the union. On May 1, the day that the council appointed a committee to draft the national petition, the L.W.M.A., which likewise met on Tuesdays, adopted an outline of the association's proposed bill for parliamentary democracy, or Charter, to be sub-

mitted to Parliament by M.P.s friendly to the society. Hetherington offered to print copies of the document without charge if the
association would provide the paper, and his offer was accepted;
a delay was occasioned, however, when Lovett gave notice of an
address to be attached to the bill, promising to have it ready the
following week. On May 8, the day that Douglas informed the
council that the preparation of the national petition had been
completed, the L.W.M.A. adopted Lovett's address and cleared
the way for the Charter to be printed. The date of the approval of
Lovett's address, May 8, 1838, later appeared in the pamphlet
edition of the Charter and has since been regarded as the date of
publication. Actually, Hetherington procrastinated and as late as
May 22 he had not yet printed the document, a failure for which
he was formally reprimanded by the association.[20] By this time
the council had presented the union's national petition to the Birmingham meeting and were preparing to take it to Glasgow and
launch a great campaign in its behalf.

Formal contact between the two societies on the subject of
their documents occurred when the council sent the L.W.M.A. a
copy of the petition in an effort to enlist the Londoners' support.
Lovett's society at this point was in danger of being upstaged,
and the best that it could do now was to intrude into the union's
agitation with its own document. On May 15, a few days before
the Glasgow meeting, the association instructed Dr. Wade and
Thomas Murphy to obtain a proof of the pamphlet and to take it
to Scotland.[21] It also sent copies to leading members of the council of the union, although it is not clear whether the union's delegation to Glasgow received them before leaving Birmingham on
the afternoon of the 17th—Douglas indicated later that he had
seen a copy of the Charter for the first time at Glasgow.[22] The
significance of these efforts by each society to get the other to
adopt its document and to get the writ placed before the public
lies not in who gained unrivaled priority, for neither succeeded in
doing so, but rather in the fact that the association had to project
itself into the union's campaign to secure an equal hearing for the
bill. The tactics of the movement clearly originated with the
council.

The meeting at Birmingham on May 14 offered comparatively
little spectacle to the public and attendance accordingly was

slight. Increasing the flatness of the event was the absence of several of the main orators of previous meetings, including Attwood, who peevishly declined to come. But the council still managed to transact the main business with pomp. Douglas read his committee's draft of the petition and it was adopted "as a proper and fitting form of a National Petition"; later the trades' leader Watson was brought forward to move that a delegation go to Glasgow and assist by their presence and counsel the great demonstration there on May 21 for the "vindication of the rights of the people and the removal of their manifold sufferings."[23]

Three days afterward, the delegates, Attwood, Salt, Douglas, P. H. Muntz, and Edmonds, set forth on the mission which, according to Douglas, might have effects to be felt a thousand years hence. There was some fear that Attwood would not participate, but he arrived late and caught up with the others at Manchester. The five men reached Hamilton, eleven miles from Glasgow, on Sunday afternoon, May 20, and were met by members of the committees of arrangement from Glasgow and Paisley. That evening a conference took place in which the Birmingham visitors approved of the schedule of events and the Scottish reformers approved of the national petition. The project of a national convention of representatives of the industrious classes also was agreed to by the Scotsmen, but it was altered to prescribe that forty-nine towns each elect one deputy, the result of a mistaken belief that no more than that many deputies could legally assemble.[24]

The following morning the "Brummagem lads," as they now were familiarly called, were escorted into Glasgow to the green where the meeting was held. A cold and unremitting rain made the procession and meeting a disagreeable experience, but there were numerous bands and banners and sufficient spectacle to attract a crowd estimated variously from 15,000 to 200,000 people. Although the latter figure was wholly implausible, being double the adult population of Glasgow, numerous spectators evidently did come from the surrounding towns, drawn to the city not only by the meeting but also by a much publicized hanging that occurred earlier in the morning. The official business saw the meeting resolve to support and sign the national petition and authorize the local committee to appoint a deputy to the convention. The Birmingham visitors explained that this was the beginning of a great national movement to obtain democracy and prosperity, and that millions of people in the kingdom would hold meetings and sign the document prior to its delivery to Parliament by the convention. The movement must remain wholly legal and peaceful, they insisted—although Attwood at one point talked of standing with the Scottish agitators "to the death," and Edmonds justified the use of physical force *in extremis*. Last of all, Wade and Murphy addressed the meeting concerning the People's Charter which had been prepared by the L.W.M.A. and which, they said, would soon be introduced into Parliament. The drenched and chilled portion of the gathering hardy enough to stay until the end then quickly dispersed. In the evening the Birmingham and London delegates were entertained at a banquet which remained exceedingly cordial despite a speech by Attwood on the state of the currency. One of the final actions of the long day was a vote of thanks to Collins, who had labored so hard to arrange the proceedings and who had been given no part in them.[25]

Now that the movement had been launched so auspiciously at Glasgow, the Birmingham delegates sought to carry their agitation to the rest of Scotland before returning home. Attwood had intended to limit his own participation to Glasgow, but he was persuaded to accompany an excursion to Paisley the next day. On Wednesday he and Edmonds left for home, and the other three members of the delegation, joined by Collins and blessed with better weather, then carried the union's appeal for support of the national petition and convention to Kilmarnock, Stirling, Perth, Dundee, Dunfermline (where Salt finally held a meeting of women), and Cupar. Large, if mostly curious and silent, crowds turned out to hear them. Finally, on Sunday, May 26, the agitators arrived at Edinburgh. The reformers there had quarreled over whether to receive them, and the next day a few radicals sponsored a meeting without the cooperation of the trades and over the opposition of moderates. A meager crowd, estimated at no more than 8,000 to 12,000 persons, came to Calton Hill for the proceedings. Wade and Murphy, continuing to shadow the Birmingham agitators, appeared at the same meeting and presented the Charter.[26] In all, it was a disappointing conclusion to the

Scottish venture that had begun so impressively at Glasgow, and the Birmingham delegates, weary and hoarse, set off for home that evening uncertain of what they had accomplished during the past week.

The hope of the council was that England would emulate Glasgow and rally behind the Birmingham union by holding meetings to sanction and sign the petition and elect deputies to the convention. It was, of course, an old story, the expectation that the country would submit spontaneously to the leadership of the Birmingham union. This time the holding of a meeting outside of Birmingham for a radical program was supposed to make a difference. But it did not. In the absence of immediate contact with radical allies elsewhere the council would have to fall back upon national publicity given the Glasgow demonstration by the press if their expectations were to have even a chance of realization. Yet the unhappy fact was that the English press of all political stripes almost entirely ignored the event. In July, Attwood finally wrote *The News* and denounced the "concealment" practiced by the London newspapers, and he thereby got a copy of the national petition printed by that paper,[27] but it was too late to do any good. The truth remained that the country knew more of the murder of Eliza Grimwood and the shooting of mad Tom of Canterbury than it did of the great Glasgow demonstration. Only one or two places in England indicated an interest in the campaign as a result of the Scottish expedition. It was still possible theoretically for the council to visit the English towns and seek support directly, of course. For this purpose Collins was instructed to return from Edinburgh by way of Newcastle, and Salt stopped off at Manchester, apparently with little success.[28] The real problem was that the council's funds were totally depleted and they could not possibly hire the one hundred agents which Salt estimated would be required to establish effective contact with the country similar to what had been done at Glasgow.

Only one alternative remained if the movement was to get under way in England: the two political bodies that possessed the organization and the contacts to rouse the southern and northern parts of the country—the L.W.M.A. and the O'Connorites, respectively—would have to come forward as bona fide co-organizers of the agitation, equal in all respects to the union and leaving Birmingham responsible only for the Midlands. Fortunately for the council, both of these groups were impressed by the Scottish venture and neither knew the weakness of the union. Both now came forward to ally with the council, and under circumstances that falsely convinced the leaders of the union their moral leadership remained preeminent.

Some understanding between the union and the L.W.M.A. was an immediate necessity, since the national petition and the Charter were so similar and the two organizations seemed about to get in each other's way. The London reformers naturally were determined to have their own show in behalf of the Charter, and following the presentation of their document to the Glasgow and Edinburgh meetings they mailed copies to working men's associations throughout the country with a request for suggestions and approval prior to the final printing of the bill and the introduction of it into Parliament. On May 22, 1838, the day following the Glasgow meeting, the association voted to rescind an invitation earlier given to the union to send a delegation to London, and instead it determined to provide a demonstration of its own in the city in behalf of the Charter. A week later it sent young Henry Vincent to attend a meeting at Bath to present the Charter there, beginning an agitation in the South and Southwest. Nevertheless, an accommodation of some kind with the Birmingham union seemingly had to be attempted before the Londoners proceeded much further, and on June 12 the association asked Murphy and Vincent to go to Birmingham and see what could be done.[29]

During the preceding week the leaders of the union had taken notice, unfavorably, of the Charter. In a speech to the council and in a lead article in the *Journal*, Douglas commented critically on the copy sent by Lovett to members of the council, particularly finding fault with the inclusion of a sixth point.[30] Such sniping undoubtedly was a covert expression of the council's annoyance over the intrusion of L.W.M.A. into the union's Scottish expedition. Yet the Birmingham society unquestionably needed the assistance of its London competitor, and the council soon arrived at an understanding with Murphy and Vincent.

The problem created by the rival documents was settled sensibly by agreeing that the national petition would be conveyed to Parliament by the convention as a first act, to demonstrate the determination of the people to have democracy, and then immediately afterward the Charter would be introduced into the House of Commons by reformer M.P.s as a means of forcing the legislators to debate and vote on the democratic program. Attwood was to lay the petition before the House of Commons and John Fielden was to introduce the bill. Each society agreed to endorse the other's document publicly in the large meeting each was planning for its own city, and each promised also to refer to both documents when attending other meetings in its region.[31] At the council's request, the L.W.M.A. subsequently consented to postpone its demonstration in London until after the union had held its giant meeting at Birmingham, now set for August 6. The association also promised to join Birmingham and Glasgow in soliciting signatures to the petition, but it indicated that it would not begin its efforts in this respect until after the meeting in London.[32] From all of these evidences of a willingness on the part of the L.W.M.A. to join in the campaign as organized by the union, the council concluded that the Londoners were prepared "to go along with Birmingham." The dream of having huge numbers from the metropolis meet delegates of the union at Hampstead Heath in a dramatic show of allegiance to the council had to be abandoned, but the "faithful assistance" of the L.W.M.A. at this juncture seemed to be the next best thing.

Simultaneous with the accord apparently reached with the Londoners was that which the union seemingly arrived at with O'Connor and his followers in the North. This entente with the Northerners was a somewhat surprising development, for O'Connor was not the kind to ally on equal terms with anybody. For some months the Irish demagogue had been mounting a campaign in Yorkshire and Lancashire in conjunction with the Rev. Joseph Stephens and Richard Oastler against the new Poor Law, an agitation in which O'Connor talked guardedly of physical force and in which the other two men openly employed threats of violence. As the agitation spread to the surrounding districts, the old radical demand for universal suffrage also figured in the meetings and in the columns of O'Connor's newspaper at Leeds. In April, O'Connor suddenly and boldly moved to gain control of the working men's associations in the North by founding a Great Northern Union which would welcome informal affiliation by all radical political societies on the basis of a vaguely stated set of principles.[33] The Leeds W.M.A. cooperated in the establishment of the new society, evidence both of O'Connor's aims and of the probability of his succeeding in them. It was clear by now that the Irishman was becoming a political force to be reckoned with in the North, but until June neither he nor the council took much notice publicly of each other, the council unquestionably hoping to by-pass him in their movement and he in turn treating the unionists with the disdain that radicals always feel for moderates.

After the successful Glasgow demonstration the Northern agitator apparently decided that he could no longer ignore the new advocates of democracy. Collins's and Salt's presence in Newcastle and Manchester left no doubt that the council hoped to expand their influence into O'Connor's own territory. On June 2, the *Northern Star* broke its near silence on the activity of the Birmingham unionists by belatedly describing the Glasgow meeting. Although the account carefully gave credit for the venture to Attwood and the "men of Birmingham" rather than to the council, the report indicated a change in policy. Simultaneously, invitations were extended to the Birmingham leaders to attend a dinner at Manchester on June 4 planned by the radicals of the North to honor John Fielden; Douglas received a special invitation to meet with the editors of the *Northern Star*, the *Northern Liberator* of Newcastle, the *Manchester Advertiser*, and several of the London weeklies "to try to agree on a uniform plan of obtaining for the people their rights." The Birmingham leaders, however, cautiously stayed away.[34] On the day following this banquet, at a meeting at Leeds to proclaim publicly the formation of the Great Northern Union, O'Connor made explicit his willingness to cooperate with the Birmingham reformers. Collins appeared on behalf of the union to present the Birmingham plan of campaign, and O'Connor declared in response (according to the *Northern Star*) that the national petition "bore the imprint of the manly Attwood and his manly followers, and let them [the audience] then and there swear allegiance to their leaders" —words that a correspondent to the *Journal* reported more exactly as "allegiance to Mr. Attwood and the men of Birmingham."

It was a flattering offer of alliance which the council had little choice but to accept, there being no real possibility of organizing an effective agitation in the North without O'Connor's assistance. "It said much for Mr. O'Connor," one of the councilmen stated at their next session, "that he should thus give up every view that might tend to divide the people, and freely consent to follow the council."[35] The difficulty with the offer, apart from the fact that it did not refer to the council directly, was the extreme aggressiveness of O'Connor and his associates and the complications of having them as allies. At the dinner at Manchester, for example, Fielden and O'Connor hinted that revolution would be justified to repeal the Poor Law, and Stephens declared that there were 5,000 guns secretly stored near Ashton, and that he wished there were fifty times that number, a near treasonous statement which Douglas mildly censured in the *Journal* a few days later.[36] Even O'Connor's pledge at Leeds to follow Attwood and the men of Birmingham had its disquieting aspects, for the same crowd that responded loudly to that affirmation of loyalty later in the meeting "rent the air" with applause and "darkened the atmosphere" with hats in declaring that they would follow Feargus to the death. A clause in the declaration of objects of the Great Northern Union established by this meeting expressly advocated physical force "in the event of moral force failing."[37] Still later in the week, at a meeting at Saddleworth attended by Collins and O'Connor together, Stephens made a speech which, although presented moderately in the *Northern Star,* actually declared that the only question before them was when to "commence burning and destroying." Collins reported back to the council that he personally had denounced the use of such language. Yet Collins also expressed his conviction that O'Connor "had given up all ideas of separate plans, and was ready and willing to go hand in hand with the men of Birmingham," and he advocated a reliance upon the Northern leader's promise to solicit signatures to the national petition and to back the abstinence project even to the extent of garrisoning the towns of Yorkshire and Lancashire.[38] The recommendation was accepted.

The alliance between the Birmingham union, the London

Working Men's Association, and the Great Northern Union was politically logical but doctrinally unsound. From the standpoint of political tactics it made good sense. The new movement could not be grounded on local agitation in the way that the drive for the reform bill had been: the appeal now was to the working classes, and since their spokesmen in most places were radicals who were suspect in the eyes of all other factions, it was virtually impossible to attract the money, publicity, and cooperation necessary for effective local petitioning and electoral action against Parliament. An alternative was regional agitation through alliances of the major organizations advocating democracy, a movement in which the reduction in local strength theoretically would be offset by regional class action. The new pattern of agitation perhaps could be accomplished if each organization stirred up the working classes in its own area.

Yet there was an obstacle to this cooperation. The three allies did not share the same philosophy in advocating democracy. The L.W.M.A. vaguely subscribed to Utilitarianism, at least as much as Francis Place could influence it to do so. This brand of Radicalism held that political education was the key to eventual success. The O'Connorite radicals, in contrast, appealed directly to the growing class consciousness of the workers, largely eschewing philosophical arguments. Lurking behind their aggressive words was the threat of violence. Both they and the Radicals of London accepted the Birmingham union's tactic of moral action only as a first stage, as something that probably would not work but that could inaugurate their own activities. In the case of the union's national petition and the L.W.M.A.'s Charter, the two strategies were compatible enough to be tied together; but the Northerners' talk of physical force potentially was a violent alternative awaiting the failure of moral action. The myth upon which the council had launched the present campaign thus underwent still another modification, for outside of the unionist camp moral action now had become merely a tentative first stage to other schemes of operation.

The acquisition of these southern and northern allies severely restricted the supervisory role the council could exercise in the national movement, and so for the time being about all that they could do independently of their new comrades in arms was to fall back upon their old myth and make the "grand Midland demonstration" a model for all the kingdom. By that means they might assert the union's moral leadership over everybody. "The crisis of their great moral warfare was at hand," Salt declared, and the people of the Midlands

> . . . must show by their attendance their determination to act, and move with, and at the command of Birmingham. They would prove to the enemies of the people that they did possess power. They must show them that all the power which Mr. O'Connor possessed in the North was at the command of the Union. That all the power of the London Working Men's Association was at the command of the Union.[39]

The idea that a large meeting at Birmingham somehow demonstrated the council's influence over all of Britain, however, was precisely the fiction that the Birmingham leaders professed to have abandoned at the start of the present movement. The fallacy of this reasoning soon was to be exposed anew.

CHAPTER VIII

Chartism and the Finale
of the Union
August 1838–April 1839

WHEN AN EXPEDITION sets unobtainable goals or employs unworkable tactics, the moment must come when the participants have to admit to the possibility of failure. Timid men then will see no reason for going on, whereas the more aggressive crusaders will insist on proceeding as a test of righteousness and, to "safeguard" the cause, almost certainly will seize control of the movement. The Chartist drive for democracy was to come to this moment of truth at a remarkably early stage—within a year the council and the L.W.M.A. were to acknowledge defeat and lose control to the aggressive Northerners—with the result that the union's active participation in the Chartist movement was to be brief and, from the standpoint of the council, disastrous.

These difficulties lay ahead. In August 1838, the council still claimed formal direction of the movement and they viewed the forthcoming Midland demonstration as a means of asserting their moral leadership. Once again Attwood's assistance seemed to be required, and the committee planning the demonstration delayed a final decision until the president of the union could be consulted. Attwood came to Birmingham for a session of the council on July 10 and was delighted, he reported, at "the reception of my faithful *Buttons*. They were like 500 *Rosabels*, clinging around me." He and the committee quickly agreed to hold the meeting on August 6 at the waste ground at Holloway Head in the southern part of the city. A week later the full council approved the plan and issued an appeal to the Midland region to respond, "a

Call which," Attwood wrote, "I trust, will shake the Temple of *Baal*, to its foundations."[1]

Many preparations had to be made during the three weeks before the meeting. The committee in Birmingham to secure signatures to the national petition spurred its efforts to garner names as preliminary proof of the enthusiasm of the people for the campaign, and by the end of July it reported about 50,000 signatures—half of what had been hoped for by this time, but still a respectable showing. Money was needed also, because the great meetings were expensive; yet all efforts to increase enrollment in and subscriptions to the union once again proved futile, with fewer than 3,000 tickets of membership being issued. The trades readily agreed to participate, and Salt acted to secure the presence of women by calling a meeting of them on the Friday preceding the demonstration. At the end of this meeting Salt suggested that his audience continue their activity by forming themselves into a female political union, a recommendation which, a critic reported, produced "the most enthusiastic screaming."[2]

More crucial for the success of the demonstration than the outcome of these local preparations were the endeavors of the council to obtain the cooperation of the neighboring towns. It was a belated effort, for the leaders of the union were weary and needed to concentrate on their businesses following the Scottish campaign; they had done no more political itinerating, even in the adjoining districts, until the end of July. During the fortnight before the demonstration, however, the councilmen revived their efforts and visited most of the towns around Birmingham to solicit their cooperation.[3] The official account they gave of their reception was "very cheering," and Attwood reported with amusement his conversation with a stranger who "told me that 'everybody within 20 miles of Birmingham was *bit by* Attwood, & that there was no doubt that he was *mad*!!!' "[4] But the following spring Salt and others revealed that their visits had not been very successful after all. The middle classes had turned a deaf ear to their appeals, the workers had been relatively unresponsive because of the railway boom and the prosperity in the region's iron industry, and the whole endeavor had been a catalogue of frustrations.[5] The meeting at Birmingham still was billed as a grand Midland demonstration, but the faithful battalions from outside of the city who had swollen the Newhall Hill meetings in the early 1830s no longer responded. The new format of the union worked no obvious magic in the towns outside of Birmingham.

Two items of business for the meeting had to be settled at the last moment following the arrival of delegates from other cities. On the evening of August 5, the spokesmen for the union gathered at P. H. Muntz's house and conferred with O'Connor, Moir, Purdie, and Vincent. The matters to be considered were a change in the plan for selecting deputies to the convention and a proposal to raise a "national rent" with which to support the work of the assembly when it convened. The council expressed a concern that fewer than forty-nine towns might elect and support individual deputies to the convention—thus far only about a half-dozen had committed themselves to do so—and therefore that the assembly might fail for lack of members. The visiting leaders agreed that such a danger must be averted and they unanimously consented to Birmingham's having eight deputies, provided that other large towns also would be entitled to multiple representation. In contrast to this unanimity, the proposal to collect a national subscription met with opposition. Both Attwood and O'Connor argued that the collection and expenditure of large sums of money might create unnecessary suspicions and dissensions; but Douglas and others on the council contended successfully that a lack of ready finances would hamper the effectiveness of the convention and might give undue influence to a few affluent deputies.[6] What went unsaid was that O'Connor, with his large income from the *Northern Star*, would have been one of these more fortunate leaders.

The council's past good luck with the weather continued unchanged. The morning of the grand demonstration was wet, but later the sky cleared and remained so until dusk. Shortly after twelve o'clock the procession to the ground at Holloway Head got under way, preceded by a band of volunteer musicians and consisting of the councilmen, visiting delegates, various trades, reformers who had arrived from surrounding towns, and finally, by two carts loaded with women. The number of bands participating in the meeting apparently was fewer than on former occasions, but there was a profusion of new flags and banners containing mottoes described by a Conservative onlooker as "seditiously appropriate." The field itself had the appearance of the Newhall Hill meetings, countless booths of venders having sprung up during the past two days, presenting, Salt admitted, a poor case for his abstinence project. The conjuring of the old myth and the strong support of the trades had produced considerable excitement, and thus the spectacle, although below previous standards, was quite adequate to attract a large crowd which numbered somewhere between the 10,000 to 20,000 estimates of the local Conservative newspapers and the 250,000 to 300,000 computations of the *Journal* and the *Northern Star*.[7] The latter figures far exceeded the total adult population of Birmingham and the surrounding region and demonstrated to what illogical extremes agitators could be led in their belief that big meetings must be followed by claims of still bigger ones.

Attwood presided, and he opened the meeting by having the audience recite a prayer, the effect of which, he wrote his wife, "was magnificently sublime."[8] He then went on to justify the movement and to advocate anew his proposal of a "sacred week" of idleness from work in the event of a rejection of the national petition. His continued refusal to accept Salt's plan of abstinence must have been an embarrassment for the lampmaker, and the difficulty of the divergence in strategy became more acute later in the meeting when O'Connor endorsed a third plan whereby 300,000 to 400,000 men would gather in London to deliver the petition and ensure its acceptance. Perhaps this uncertainty over what to do if the petition failed to get a hearing, plus competition exerted by the presence of O'Connor, accounts for the unusually aggressive speeches made by most of the councilmen. Attwood set the tone by declaring that he preferred to act peaceably, "but woe unto the man who breaks the law against us." P. H. Muntz asserted that 200,000 arms had commanded success in 1832 and "Were they not as well prepared to act in 1838 as in 1832?" Edmonds again defended the possible use of physical force; and even Salt got into the act by saying that if the House of Commons refused to do the people justice, "they would hear another and a louder clap of thunder, and that would be the last." O'Connor also used strong words, including a citation of the fourth chapter of Lamentations, "where it is stated that it is better to be slain by the sword than to perish by famine," but the council had stolen his thunder. They were to regret their accomplishment a few months later when the Irish agitator turned their statements against them.

The meeting efficiently dispatched the business put before it. Eight councilmen were named as deputies from Birmingham to the convention—G. F. and P. H. Muntz, Douglas, Salt, Hadley, Pierce, Edmonds, and Collins. Resolutions granted these eight men the power to call together the "General Convention of the Industrious Classes" and *ad interim* to collect the national rent and signatures to the national petition. In compliance with the promise made to the L.W.M.A., the council also had the meeting vote its approval of the Charter as the outline of an act to provide for the just representation of the people, "agreeably to the principles set forth in the *National Petition*." By now the showers of the morning had returned and the crowd soon afterward began to scatter.[9] The council intended this to be the last great Birmingham meeting to be sponsored by the union, and in this anticipation they were to prove correct, although not for the advantageous reasons which they envisioned.

Because the establishment of the convention now seemed assured, and the council's plan called for the deputies upon assembling to take formal command of the movement, the leaders of the union could begin to relax after the meeting, secure in the feeling that responsibility for the fate of the country soon would rest partly upon other shoulders. Even the major publicity given the demonstration by the London and provincial press, although welcome, no longer seemed so vital to the cause. The council duly condemned the *Weekly Dispatch* for its adverse remarks, to be sure, but they did so on the ground that the editor was an apostate Radical and, as Salt had declared, "doubt was treachery" once the movement got under way.[10] Another obvious cause for the council's relaxation was the shift of the spotlight now to their new allies, who had to prove themselves equal in moral leadership to the council by matching the union's large Birmingham meeting with great demonstrations in their own territories.

Ironically, it was not until this time, when the leaders of the union viewed the organization's role as diminishing, that the make-up of the council finally assumed a broader, more democratic basis. At the annual election preceding the demonstration no less than seven workingmen came onto the council, including the trades' leaders Watson and Baker, and there was only one addition from the middle class. Soon after this date, however, the newly elected Birmingham deputies to the convention began to hold separate meetings of their own, and attendance by them and others on the council fell off sharply. Watson complained bitterly that he at last had been admitted to the council, only to have the others ignore him. In their meetings the deputies meanwhile arranged for the receipt from elsewhere in the country of signatures made to the national petition, names of deputies elected by other places, and reports of contributions made to the national rent.[11] Compared to these matters the routine business of the council now seemed unimportant.

A duty that again took the union leaders into territory outside of the Midlands was their obligation to return the visit their allies had made to Birmingham for the union's August 6 meeting. Lovett and the L.W.M.A. had their own demonstration in London scheduled for September 17, and O'Connor and his followers had great meetings planned for after that date at Manchester, Liverpool, and the West Riding; naturally delegates from the council were expected to be present. Both the council and their sponsors viewed these meetings as a test of the momentum of the drive for democracy because it was believed that the areas around the big cities would not stir except by the example of urban centers, or as it was put more affirmatively by Douglas, "As certain as the gravity physical of the sun retained the planets in their respective orbits, would the gravity moral of the large towns gather round and regulate the small ones, and constrain them to obey."[12] The Birmingham leaders therefore could not fail to desire success for these key meetings elsewhere, although they did not wholly repress the annoyance they felt at the independence, the absence of any hint of moral vassalage, exhibited by the Londoners and the Northerners in the staging of the demonstrations.

Douglas and P. H. Muntz went as delegates to the London meeting. Douglas earlier had pettishly complained that the large number of other societies invited to send delegates to London made the presence of Birmingham men unnecessary, but he attended anyway and made a modest and appropriate speech saying that he represented the "Brummagem buttons" who desired unity among all reformers. Muntz took no part in the proceedings.[13] A week later, in response to a promise made personally to R. J. Richardson, secretary of the Manchester Political Union, a contingent from the council journeyed to Manchester to attend the demonstration held on Kersal Moor on September 24. Douglas, Collins, and Pierce participated, and Salt attended but did not speak.[14] The following day Collins traveled to Liverpool and joined Edmonds in representing the union at the demonstration sponsored by the O'Connorite forces there.[15] Finally, after an interval of slightly over a fortnight, Collins went to Yorkshire as a delegate from the union to the West Riding demonstration held at Hartshead Moor on October 15.[16] The reports to the council upon their return from the four meetings reveal a pattern of deteriorating relations with their allies: Muntz and Douglas reported after the London meeting that "the most perfect uniformity of opinion" existed between the Radicals of London and Birmingham; the delegates to the Manchester and Liverpool demonstrations returned with some words of praise for the other speakers but with no affirmations of solidarity; and Collins came back from his solitary journey to the West Riding meeting with mild praise for its organizers, only to be drowned out by criticism of the event voiced by Douglas and others who had stayed home.[17]

These weeks indeed marked a turning point in the movement. The fragile alliance of the three camps of reformers, as yet barely cemented, began to come apart as soon as the frustrations and irritations of campaigning exposed their underlying differences. The initial and most fundamental cause of trouble was the emergence of signs that the movement as a moral endeavor might fail to get very far. The plan of campaign projected an avalanche of meetings, triggered by several huge demonstrations in key places and culminating in the presentation of the national petition bearing millions of signatures. A slackening anywhere in the movement could be interpreted as a sign that the drive as a whole was losing its force. This possibility now arose to disturb the reformers. According to the participants' own statements, for example, the demonstration in London attracted at most 12,000 to 15,000 persons,[18] fewer than what a boxing match at Greenwich drew at the same hour and a far cry from the million people the council had envisioned earlier. It was a performance hardly calculated to excite the metropolis itself, much less the surrounding area, and without finances in hand—the L.W.M.A. was even poorer than the Birmingham union—the best that Lovett and his associates could do in the South and Southwest was to appeal to the associations for support and then send Vincent to two or three selected places to stir up the people.[19]

In the North, the organizers of the Manchester demonstration claimed greater success, estimating attendance at their meeting at anywhere from 200,000 persons up to O'Connor's fantastic figure of 500,000 men, ten times the adult male population of the city. Even the critics of the affair conceded attendance of 30,000 or more. The Liverpool demonstration the following day, however, was a dismal failure by the reformers' own admission, with calculations of attendance ranging only from 1,200 to 5,000 persons.[20] Nor did the West Riding demonstration the following month come up to expectations.[21] By this time it was evident that there would be no avalanche and that the meetings held in smaller towns would have to result generally from direct action by visiting agitators rather than from the exciting example of three or four urban centers.

The council's own experience in the Midlands seemed to confirm this impression of a faltering movement. The neighboring towns that had failed to send their thousands to the Birmingham demonstration on August 6 now failed to conduct agitation on their home ground. At Kidderminster, Salt, Hadley, and Douglas attempted to get up a meeting and were forced to retire when Tory opponents almost precipitated a riot; at Wolverhampton similar difficulties apparently prevented Salt from speaking.[22] A meeting to organize agitation at Coventry attended by Salt and Pierce, one at Stratford-on-Avon attended by Emes, and one at Nuneaton attended by Hadley and Douglas all bore little fruit.[23] Most of the other towns in the area did not hold meetings. The result was that when the convention convened a few months later all of Warwickshire outside of Birmingham, the whole of Worcestershire, and all of Staffordshire south of the Potteries had contributed fewer than 20,000 signatures to the national petition and almost nothing to the national rent.[24] Farther afield, Salt and Pierce represented the union at a meeting at Sheffield in September, Salt journeyed to Nottingham and Loughborough in November, and Pierce visited the Potteries the same month; but the council's enthusiasm had wholly waned by the latter occasion and none of them showed up at a meeting at Leicester a fortnight later, despite previous assurances that a delegation would be present.[25] Thereafter no further meetings in the Midlands were attended by members of the council.

The frustrations associated with these signs of possible collapse did not fail to increase the suspicions and animosities already existing in the ranks of the reformers. The council's chief grievance against Lovett's group was that the L.W.M.A. emphasized the Charter in its agitation almost to the exclusion of the national petition. The council should have expected this, but as a consequence of the neglect the metropolis produced only 19,000 signatures to the petition and only £15 to the national rent by the time the convention met. All of the rest of the South and Southwest added only 7,245 signatures and £30.[26] The council's annoyance was such that they might have severed all ties between the union and the L.W.M.A. at this time had O'Connor not antagonized both societies sufficiently to keep them allied in what Salt called the party "of sense and discretion" against "the Brawlers."[27]

From the start the relationship of the Birmingham and London moderates with the O'Connorites was taxing, for the two sides had a deep-seated distrust of each other. The Northern demagogue in fact usually disregarded the two moderate societies and referred to his allies only as "the men of Birmingham" and "the London operatives." In his speeches he seldom mentioned the People's Charter, and the *Northern Star* never published the document; the national petition received his attention instead, but he usually spoke vaguely of its principles and not of the need to sign it. Because he was not favorable to the idea of a national rent, he simply ignored it, a tactic reflected later in the failure of Newcastle, Manchester, and the West Riding to report any collection whatever. Repeatedly he warned his hearers to watch the Birmingham leaders carefully for any evidence of backsliding to an interest in the currency issue, yet he made no effort to persuade Stephens, Oastler, and others in his camp to cease agitating against the Poor Law. Even more galling, he increasingly claimed personal credit for the creation of the present movement, and he suggested that his alliance with the Birmingham union was possible only because the members of the union had forced the council to abandon Whiggery. Occasionally he feigned humility and talked of being merely a drummer in Attwood's and Fielden's army, but his hearers knew better.

All of these irritations, bothersome as they were, might have been tolerable if O'Connor had agitated exclusively in his own territory. But with an inherent distrust of the moderates to the south and with money and abundant publicity available from the *Northern Star,* he could not resist the temptation to range far afield. He was exceptionally gifted with demagogic assets— imposing size, booming voice, rough humor, and limitless supply of invective—all of which made him a favorite with working-class audiences. His appeal to the class consciousness of the workers freed him from the entanglements and restrictions of philosophies. He could intrude into any meeting confident of being the star performer. He seemed tireless in his ability to travel and speak, and he attended dozens of meetings in the North before coming to the Birmingham meeting of August 6, permitting him to claim that he was there as the representative of "the wishes and feelings of 3,000,000 of determined minds and stalwart arms."[28] Included in his itinerary, most of which was given to advocating the cause of his Northern Union, was a tour of Scotland in July, and thus he came to Birmingham as a delegate from some of the very places that the council had agitated in May. Later in August he advanced into the Midlands itself, speaking first at Stratford-on-Avon and Coventry, and then at the town hall in Birmingham. This last engagement took place without any consultation with the council and at the same hour at which the Birmingham leaders were scheduled to meet, even though he had been given the floor for a lengthy speech when he had visited the council the week before. Still, the council had no choice but to adjourn their own session and join the admiring crowd attending the Irishman at the town hall.[29]

On September 17 it was the L.W.M.A.'s turn to be irritated, for O'Connor showed up at the London demonstration claiming to have been delegated by almost the entire North, and in effect informing everyone that the working men's associations outside the South were in his own pocket. He obviously was prepared to throw his weight around, but he lost most of his opportunity to do so when the L.W.M.A. warily left his London followers off the program. The next month he was back, complaining of the "base and sneaking opposition by which he had been formerly cramped in his exertions" and making arrangements with the democratic association there for new agitation to advance his position.[30] On his return north he stopped off unannounced at Birmingham to attend the council again, but this time Douglas gave him no publicity in the *Journal,* explaining crisply that the proceedings of the session were "uninteresting."[31] In November the Northern leader once more returned to the Midlands to attend meetings at the Potteries and at Leicester. By this time the council and the L.W.M.A. had begun to suspect, correctly, that their ally would not hesitate in the event of a dispute to take over the whole movement.

Control of the meetings that appointed deputies to the convention was a source of future power in the movement. The council had naively assumed that the convention somehow would be an extension of their own will because they had originated the idea of having it. Thus they had preached the doctrine of absolute obedience by the industrious classes to the convention's dictates. "With a tyrant's power and with a father's love," Douglas had proclaimed, "the convention must reign and rule, unopposed, unchallenged, till the great day of the deliverance comes."[32] All of this must have seemed excellent so long as moderates such as the Birmingham councilmen themselves were chosen as deputies. The L.W.M.A., too, took care to see that mostly its own were nominated at the metropolitan demonstration. In the North, however, events went differently: O'Connor ceaselessly campaigned against the election of "sham-Radicals" and he got his supporters chosen at the Manchester, Liverpool, and West Riding demonstrations. Among these radicals were Stephens, Richardson, and O'Brien. With more elections to follow and with other violent men certain to be picked, it was clear that there would be a major party of O'Connorites in the convention, determined to have their way.

The growing rivalry among the reformers raised with greater urgency the problem of what to do if the legislature rejected the national petition. Each of the camps had its pet formula or formulas, soon called "ulterior measures," to ensure success in such a situation, yet in each case the rival agitators had little difficulty in pointing out weaknesses in each other's plans. Salt's abstinence scheme, for example, presupposed a national unity of purpose among the working classes which did not exist, and the lampmaker himself admitted that, although the women might give up their tea, it was questionable whether the men would forgo ale and tobacco; in any case O'Connor and others doubted that a temporary drop in revenue would bring the government to its knees. Attwood's proposal of a general strike depended upon the masters "shaking hands" with the workers and supporting them in the venture by continuing their wages, a most unlikely development indeed. The L.W.M.A. wanted the reformers to renew their petitioning effort over and over on the theory that each rejection of the document would swell the demand for it until eventually Parliament would have to pass the Charter as a means of stopping the petitioning; but Salt and others were quick to observe that repeated defeat seldom generates increased enthusiasm and determination. O'Connor's idea of having a half million men deliver the petition to Parliament was nothing more than Irish bravado which did not answer the question of what to do if the legislature spurned the document, and which ignored the probability that the ministers would use military force to counter a threatening march. Richardson and a few agitators in Manchester talked of a run on gold, but now that Place and the Westminster Radicals were turning their attention from democracy to the corn laws the scheme was not echoed elsewhere; anyway it was the middle classes and skilled workers who had the savings to withdraw from banks, not the poorer laborers. In short, no constitutional proposal for action had yet been advanced that seemed likely under the circumstances of a faltering movement to accomplish very much.

What, then, of unconstitutional action? Soon all of the mutual suspicions and grievances of the rival reformers centered on the question of physical force, even though none of the agitators claimed explicitly to advocate it. The real issue was how far reformers should go in raising a threat of violence without actually resorting to or inciting it. Here the factions divided sharply, for the O'Connorite forces seemed almost to welcome the possibility of violence, provided that it was a spontaneous act by the working classes and did not directly implicate themselves, whereas the Birmingham and London reformers were not disposed to risk bloodshed at all. An embarrassment for the council were the numerous occasions on which they had pleased their audiences by employing strong words and talk of force in self-defense, but the catch was that they had not genuinely meant what they said. Aggressive oratorical flourishes had seemed harmless enough as long as moral force was judged certain to work, but once there appeared a real possibility of the collapse of peaceful strategy the council came to regard as dangerous the use of any language that was likely to encourage disturbances.

Until autumn the Birmingham leaders hid their misgivings and chose to overlook the violent words of their allies to the north, hard though it was to ignore the "blood for blood" speeches and writings of Stephens and Oastler against the new Poor Law. The closest that they came to censuring the Northerners was their intimation that O'Connor sometimes was "impolitic" and their suggestion that Stephens's and Oastler's reason may have become "clouded" by a passion for justice. O'Connor's argument that the Northerners' talk of physical force was merely "theoretical" seemed to be accepted by the union's leaders whether or not it was actually believed. By mid-October, however, the petitioning movement appeared to be flagging and the intemperate words sounded more ominous. The uneasiness felt by the Birmingham and London leaders increased still more when O'Connor organized nighttime, torch-light meetings in retaliation against masters who would not release their workers to attend meetings during the day. The publicity given the movement in the nation's press meanwhile increased almost proportionately to the sharpness of the language used at the meetings, seemingly justifying the new tactics among the O'Connorites, but merely heightening the concern felt by the council and the L.W.M.A. that the movement was getting out of hand.

In a lead article on October 20, 1838, Douglas complained that O'Connor no longer seemed to be interested in obtaining signatures to the national petition. Taking note of the "strong speaking" prevalent in the North, he declared that "We really had hoped that the men of Birmingham had cooled down this extravagance of diction." His mild reproof had no effect, for O'Connor and Stephens continued to talk of "the right" of the people to arm and fight. The following week at a session of the council Douglas denounced the use of arms "repeatedly and pointedly alluded to by leading characters in the present movement." The question was not whether the people had a legal right to buy firearms, he declared, but whether it was illegal to incite men to use them against the government. Furthermore, he added, if the radical agitators really wanted an uprising they would be the most insane of fools to tell the government of their intentions. Salt followed, and attacked O'Connor by name, saying that the Irishman had continually assured him in private that he was an apostle of peace and yet he publicly advocated the use of force. The remarks of Douglas and Salt appeared in the *Journal* and of course were promptly called to the attention of the men against whom they were directed. Stephens answered with more violent speeches, exhorting an audience at Norwich to "fight with swords, fight with pistols, fight with daggers, fight with your torches" in a "war to the knife, so help me God!" — words that were quoted by Douglas at the next session of the council in demanding that Stephens withdraw as a deputy to the convention. O'Connor reacted to the criticism by declaring that he would go to Birmingham and allow the people there to choose between him and Salt. Rather than retracting anything he had said, he set September 29 of the following year as the date beyond which he would no longer continue peaceful exertions.[33] A showdown seemed at hand.

The clash that followed between O'Connor and the council extended over a fortnight and on the surface appeared to end satisfactorily for the Birmingham leaders. Because most of the council apparently had not learned of O'Connor's challenge prior to their session on November 13, Salt and several other spokesmen were out of town or otherwise engaged when the Irishman first showed up to do battle. A minor confrontation took place between O'Connor and Collins at this session, and upon Collins's insistence that the convention alone could set a date for the termination of peaceful agitation O'Connor surprisingly backed down and said that he would wait and propose the matter to the convention. The decisive event, however, was the reception given O'Connor by the gallery, "the jury" to whom he had brought his appeal. The visitor's demagogic talents quickly won them over, and their repeated cheers for him and their cries of "shame" when he read Salt's criticism left little doubt about who would be the victor when he returned the following week.[34] In a test of strength it was clear that O'Connor's appeal to class action was stronger than the council's revamped myth, even in Birmingham itself.

During the days before O'Connor's return the council sought Attwood's assistance, and the ailing president of the union obliged with a letter to the members repeating his old exhortations and warnings. He asserted that the "moral tempest" raised by the Birmingham union was "at this moment howling around the battlements of the government, and shaking the tabernacles of fraud, cruelty, and oppression," and he declared that the source of the union's power still was an adherence to strict legality. He then advanced the argument, afterward repeatedly stated by the council in their opposition to physical force, that if the people did not possess sufficient discipline to effect peaceful "ulterior measures" they certainly would not endure the privations necessary to win a revolution. The council publicized the letter, and meanwhile they continued their volleying at Stephens, being further exasperated when the Northern firebrand contemptuously dismissed them as "foolish old women." And they directed their fire on Oastler as well, with Douglas declaring that the former Thornhill steward was a man of the most ungoverned temper and ungoverned tongue. Yet there were also signs of a cautious withdrawal from any further confrontation with O'Connor, for both Douglas and Salt carefully distinguished between the illegal incitements to force voiced by Stephens and Oastler and the mere "fervor of enthusiasm" of which O'Connor was guilty.[35] Their opponent by this time likewise began to lean toward a truce, declaring at Leicester that his disagreement with the council was "a distinction of opinion without a difference."[36]

A formal reconciliation followed. The council's October 20 session at the public office was so besieged with members and observers that the large numbers unable to obtain entry drowned out the proceedings with their complaints and finally forced an adjournment of the "trial" until the 28th, when the town hall would be available. The crowd did not know that O'Connor and Salt already had met that morning and had agreed to debate the "principles" of their positions without personal rancor. Upon O'Connor's reappearance the following week negotiations between him and the council, conducted for the latter principally by Collins, completed the restoration of peace. Salt agreed to a resolution of apology to the offended Irishman, and O'Connor approved of a declaration condemning all exhortations to physical force. The thousands who crowded the town hall on the evening of October 28 in anticipation of a dramatic conflict were given instead resolutions affirming renewed unity.

Salt, Douglas, Hadley, Pierce, and Collins all rejoiced at what they regarded as a victory for the council's moral leadership of the movement. But was it a victory? O'Connor's acceptance of the resolution condemning an advocacy of physical force meant little, for he had never admitted to having advised the use of violence: all he had done, he maintained, was to point out the physical reality behind moral force, a reality he neither created nor controlled. The apology that he received seemingly exonerated him from any fault on this score, and the settlement in fact did not mention references to the right of arming, one of the chief issues leading to the encounter. The audience in each of the meetings "vehemently cheered" O'Connor, but greeted the council with a mixture of cheers and hisses. The Northern demagogue therefore could now well afford to be conciliatory toward his opponents because, having successfully demonstrated his influence in the very citadel of the council, he had nothing further to gain by breaking with them completely.

The two most astute politicians on the council, Edmonds and

P. H. Muntz, realized the significance of what had occurred and they provided the major excitement at the meetings when they refused to accept the rapprochement. At the council session on the 20th Edmonds denounced the fixing of a day by O'Connor and he shouted, "No, by God! he would never stand [for] it." Muntz demanded that O'Connor dissociate himself from Stephens. O'Connor replied in almost patronizing terms that he had already withdrawn his threat to set a date and that he was not responsible for Stephens's speeches. The next week Muntz angrily sent in his resignation to the council, and Edmonds took up the demand that O'Connor denounce Stephens and Oastler; he continued it on the 28th at the town hall despite efforts by the others to call him off. O'Connor in reply briefly pointed to Edmonds's own recent defense of physical force. The following week the attorney's clerk resigned from the council.[37] Muntz meanwhile was persuaded to return, but he attended only a few more sessions of the council and he refused to serve as a deputy to the convention. Other members, including Betts, also became inactive.

The withdrawals left the union leadership in the hands of the five men who still were willing to act as deputies: Salt, Douglas, Hadley, Pierce, and Collins. Undoubtedly, they were men of lesser ability than their departing associates. Of the five, Salt was the most genial and dedicated, and his personal character was much praised by other reformers; yet he had little capacity for leadership and organization. Typical of the comments about him was Douglas's instruction to Lovett to send some convention letters "to me by Mr. Hadley—*not* Mr. Salt [,] he'll forget or lose them."[38] Douglas was a more practical hand at organizing and directing things, but he was erratic and moody and, while respected, was not well-liked or trusted. Pierce was "a fourth-rate leader," in the words of a Tory editor, "ignorant and illiterate" and known mostly for his frenzied style of speaking.[39] The same comments to a lesser degree could be made of Hadley, who in fact had been relatively inactive in politics since the death of his eldest son in June and who seems to have been chosen as a deputy largely because of his long association with the union. Collins was an above average speaker and organizer, and he had the advantage of being a workingman, but the rustic simplicity, lack of education, and grave demeanor which served him well in his role as a novice agitator actually were poor credentials for the convention. To make matters worse for the union, these five men could not expect much help from the two former field marshals of the society. Attwood was in poor health and had withdrawn to the Isle of Wight to recover; also, he was preoccupied at the moment with the danger of an attack from the Russians, an event that he solemnly predicted would occur as soon as the Baltic ice melted and freed the Russian fleet. G. F. Muntz was recovering from a severe accident and was tied more than ever to his business in Wales; he came to Birmingham only occasionally, and his selection as deputy was purely honorary. The union, in short, was approaching its greatest test with less than its best commanders in the field.

During this time while the council awaited the convening of the national convention of deputies they consolidated their control over the local government of Birmingham. In November the city received its charter of incorporation, and in December the first municipal election took place. The middle-class electors, reluctant though they were to follow the council into democracy, had not abandoned their old loyalties in other respects and in the election they returned to the town council the entire list of forty-eight Radicals and Liberals recommended by the union, including eighteen present or past members of the council. The Conservatives offered opposition in every ward without success. Next, the unionists and a few Liberal allies on the town council appointed from their own ranks sixteen aldermen for six-year terms, and they made William Scholefield mayor, William Redfern town clerk, Douglas registrar, and Edmonds clerk of the peace. "With the exception of one or two water-gruel politicians," an opposing editor groaned, "the Corporation, as at present constituted, consists of the nominees or lick-spittles of the Political Union."[40] Joseph Parkes agreed: "Curse their aristocratic Bourgeois propensities."[41]

It also developed during these weeks that Muntz's and Edmonds's skepticism about the prospects for future cooperation with O'Connor was well-founded. A basis for new trouble appeared on December 5 when some Scottish moderates met at Calton Hill in Edinburgh and adopted resolutions condemning physical force in much the same terms that the council previously had used. At once O'Connor suspected collusion between these new "moral cowards" and those at Birmingham. In an address in the *Northern Star* the Irish demagogue solemnly warned the Edinburgh and Birmingham Radicals that he intended to go to Scotland to answer the charges there, and that any further sign of wavering at Birmingham would be summarily dealt with. Matters grew worse following the government's proclamation banning torchlight meetings and, a fortnight later, the arrest of Stephens for using seditious language. A chorus of angry voices immediately arose among O'Conner's followers denouncing the "shuffling and false traitors" of Birmingham, London, and Edinburgh who had created the division that allegedly had encouraged the government to act; most of the accusers did not fail to point out that it was the "old women" on the council of the Birmingham union who had first broken the reformers' ranks and endangered the cause of the people.

The council reacted to the new outburst of abuse with remarkable forbearance. Douglas expressed a cautious approval of the Edinburgh meeting and of the ban on torchlight meetings, and even of the arrest of Stephens, but he and the speakers at the sessions of the council carefully avoided any personal recriminations in noting the attacks of the Northerners on themselves. The closest they came to risking a new visit from O'Connor was Douglas's complaint that O'Connor was in the habit of making moderate statements and then offsetting them with violent ones, and his further opinion that "notwithstanding the ridiculous rhodomontade of a few itinerating spouters, the masses are not, in the smallest degree, inclined to fight." The same moderation was exhibited in speeches that Collins made in meetings at Cheltenham and Bristol and that Pierce made at Reading as delegates of the union.[42] Most of the council's pronouncements during this period consisted of warnings that if signatures to the national petition and contributions to the national rent proved as inadequate as it now appeared they would be, then the convention when it met would have no business to conduct and no money with which to conduct it.

A more decisive reaction to the fresh attack by the O'Connorites came from the members of the union. The council's departure from their policy of discouraging organizations among the members had facilitated the development: to place the task of collecting the national rent in the hands of the members themselves, the council early in December had agreed that a committee of members should be formed to oversee the effort. Soon thereafter the members met and chose twenty-one persons to constitute the proposed "National Rent Committee." The leading voices on it were the secretary, Edward Brown, described as a householder but a poor laborer; John Powell, the former council member; John Fussell, a newspaper agent and one of a family of agitators; Henry Alexander Donaldson, a cabinetmaker and upholsterer, and apparently a newcomer to Birmingham; and James Porter, a shoemaker. All five men, plus several of the lesser lights, were aggressive persons who were likely to be sympathetic to physical force arguments. Their bent of mind became evident as soon as the new breach between the council and O'Connor appeared, for the committee held a meeting and strongly backed O'Connor and Stephens. Afterward they began presiding over regular meetings of the members on Thursday evenings, and in January they abandoned to the female union most of the work of soliciting the rent in Birmingham and gave their own attention to an agitation of the surrounding towns, using for the purpose some of the money collected for the rent. The trades' spokesmen, Baker and Watson, temporized, unwilling either to join or to oppose the new activity by the workers. Obviously the council now had on their hands an aggressive rival rather than a subservient body of assistants.[43]

Fortunately for the council the union was able to escape another visitation by O'Connor during these weeks of growing internal division. Their good luck was possible in part because the Irishman was busy challenging the L.W.M.A. and the Edinburgh reformers in public meetings in London and Scotland, thus diverting attention from Birmingham. The L.W.M.A. in December had made a struggle between itself and the radicals inevitable when it adopted a resolution condemning physical force, although it did so without attacking O'Connor by name.[44] A few days later the Northern demagogue descended on the city in keeping with the pledge he had given to the democratic association two months before, and in a series of meetings he carried all before him. The showdown with Lovett came in a stormy meeting on December 20 at the Hall of Science, City Road, and not only did O'Connor win the audience to his side, he also persuaded Hetherington, Vincent, and Richard Hartwell to desert their old associates and join his camp.[45] To complete his coup, the Irishman went to Scotland early in January and engaged the moderates there in a trial of strength. In meetings at Edinburgh and Glasgow he secured resolutions "rescinding" the previous condemnation of physical force and thereby vanquished the "Scottish traitors" who had criticized him. Stopping off at Newcastle on his way home, O'Connor proclaimed triumphantly that the divisions raised in Birmingham, London, and Scotland had ended.[46]

Almost as abruptly as he had engaged his allies of August in this new test of popular strength, O'Connor in mid-January 1839 called off the hostilities. The continued participation of moderates in the movement was desirable and, having demonstrated his strength in London and Edinburgh as well as Birmingham, O'Connor once more had nothing further to gain by continuing the quarrel. His followers soon took the cue, and thus instead of unkind words there again were calls for unity and references to "our friends" of Birmingham, London, and Scotland. Indicative of the change was the extravagant praise given by the radical press to the council when the unionists successfully invaded a "subversive" meeting got up by the Liberals of Birmingham to petition for a repeal of the corn laws.[47] The council welcomed the apparent restoration of goodwill and in turn expressed the hope that the deficiency in signatures and rent which they had prophesied earlier might not be so large after all, or at least that the effect of it might be overcome, and that the convention might accomplish great things as originally planned. A few days later, when the deputies to the convention gathered in London at the British Coffee House for their initial meeting, Attwood went to greet them and he afterwards reported to his wife that "the Bir^m men came out & told me that everything was going on well; they anticipate no mischief from the *mad caps*, who appear to be a good deal tamed."[48] In the minds of the council, it would seem, wishful political thinking and moral campaigning finally had become indistinguishable.

Although the convention met for the first time on February 4, 1839, summoned by the Birmingham deputies in their capacity as an interim committee, some preliminary maneuvering already had occurred among the two rival camps of reformers. O'Connor and Richardson had convened meetings of the Northern deputies at Bury on December 8 and at Manchester on January 7 to discuss policies, and the latter meeting had sent a delegation to confer with the Birmingham deputies. Evidently this conference led to the summoning of the convention.[49] The Birmingham representatives for their part soon devised a strategy to advance the moderates' influence in the convention. They proposed to have the assembly refuse to certify deputies who came to London bearing no signatures to the petition and no contributions to the national rent. Because this rule presumably would hurt the O'Connorites most, Douglas wrote Lovett and arranged for a preliminary meeting with him and his London friends on February 3 to discuss the scheme.[50] A few days later when the sixty or so deputies from throughout Britain actually assembled, however, the Birmingham leaders grew timid and refused to fight for the regulation, perhaps because they had found no way to prevent all of the deputies present, whether with or without the credentials in question, from participating in the convention's decision on the matter. Consequently the delinquents were given a month in which to produce at least some token signatures and money.[51]

Once the convention had referred to committees such inconsequential matters as the selection of a permanent meeting place, the adoption of rules and regulations, and the preparation of an address to the people, the deputies had to turn their attention to their major, preannounced business. They had met to oversee the presentation of the national petition to Parliament, to arrange for the subsequent introduction of the Charter, and then, assuming that either the petition or the Charter would be rejected, to direct the employment of one or more "ulterior measures" to force favorable action by the legislature. Yet the very first step in their plan, the collection of at least three million signatures to a national petition demanding democracy, had not been accomplished at all. The tally of signatures, real and estimated, came to slightly over half a million, and of these only one-quarter of a million actually were in hand, the rest being merely "reported."

The concomitant campaign to raise a national rent to finance the work of the convention had netted only £967, a fraction of the £10,000 that the council had estimated would be needed.[52] It was clear therefore that the convention would have to delay the presentation of the petition until additional signatures and rent could arrive. Salt himself moved on February 6 that the deadline for the accumulation of names to the petition be extended until the 28th. Later in the week the convention took a more decisive step and decided to conduct agitation in the metropolis and to send "missionaries" into the country to hold meetings and solicit signatures and rent.[53] Because all of the Birmingham deputies except Collins had returned home before the vote on this proposal, it is not known how they viewed the matter, but strategically it must have seemed to them a very awkward action inasmuch as an overwhelming, popular demand for democracy was supposed to have brought the deputies together in the first place.

The truth was inescapable that the moral campaign as envisioned by the council had failed. The excitement incident to organizing the assembly had raised all of the deputies to high spirits during the first few days, but quickly it became evident that the talk of many hundreds of thousands of signatures and many thousands of pounds being en route to London was pure speculation. The poor results of the drive thus far naturally raised questions about the rest of the plan, and particularly whether the people would make the sacrifices necessary to implement an ulterior measure. Even the state of the economy seemed to conspire against the reformers, with a returning prosperity discernibly dampening the willingness of the working classes to agitate. Perhaps the most subtle evidence of the lack of success of the moral campaign was the growing tendency of the reformers, including even the Birmingham men, to refer to the movement predominantly in terms of the Charter, a document that was not as deeply associated with the unionist myth and with the failure of regional agitation as was the national petition.

From the viewpoint of the Birmingham deputies, there was no alternative but to admit defeat. The O'Connorites, however, now saw added reason to raise the threat of physical force. Any public statement of either of these opposing sentiments, of course, would immediately revive the quarrel between the two camps of reformers. Obviously it was an ominous portent when on Monday of the second week of the convention Richardson referred to the right of arming and drew cries of "No, no" from Douglas. That evening, during the first of the meetings to agitate the metropolis, held at the White Conduit House, most of the speakers from the North used strong language and O'Connor himself declared that "physical force was treason only when it failed; it was glorious freedom when it was successful." On Wednesday, the Irish demagogue and Douglas clashed over O'Connor's statement that Attwood had threatened to use physical force during the agitation for the reform bill.[54] Douglas went home the next day to edit the *Journal,* and when it appeared on Saturday, February 16, it contained a lead article in which the editor observed that the petition had received the sanction of not more than one-seventh of the nonelectors of Britain and that all the lungs in Christendom proclaiming success could not convert one-half million signatures into three million. The lower-class leviathan had not really awakened, he said, it merely had turned to the other side, and therefore if there was no change in the situation by the end of the month, "we really see no course open to the Convention, but an adjournment till next year, or till a more favourable season." The next day Douglas and Salt expressed these sentiments, somewhat more cautiously, in letters to Lovett asking to be excused for personal reasons from attendance at the convention for the coming week, and Salt afterward repeated the theme at a meeting of the women's union and at a session of the council.[55]

The initial attitude of the O'Connorites toward this "renewed treason" by the Birmingham deputies was surprisingly mild, consisting mainly of derision of the moderates' "lack of courage." By now the physical force advocates knew they were in the ascendancy and they could afford to be merely contemptuous rather than angry. The *Northern Star,* the *Charter,* and the *Operative* questioned Douglas's figures and censured him and his Birmingham associates, and the radicals of Manchester issued a long address answering the *Journal* "point for point,"[56] but the attacks lacked the venom of the previous rebukes. The anger of the Northerners undoubtedly was lessened also by the refusal of the Birmingham deputies to say much in reply[57] and by the decision of all except Collins to stay away from the convention.

The decision to remain home was facilitated by the inclusion of Collins, Salt, Pierce, and Hadley among the fifteen missionaries appointed by the assembly to agitate the country prior to the presentation of the petition (now postponed until May), thus giving these four men an official reason for being absent. Collins was assigned Oxfordshire, Buckinghamshire, Berkshire, and Bedfordshire, and he proceeded to the first of these and soon sent back enthusiastic reports on his efforts to rouse the people there to activity, although later he gave it up as hopeless.[58] Salt and Hadley were asked to organize Warwickshire, Worcestershire, and Staffordshire, a territory that, Salt pointed out, they already had unsuccessfully tried to agitate. The result was that the lampmaker and the buttonmaker reportedly never ventured more than a mile or so from their factories after they came home from London. Pierce, who was assigned northern Wales, simply dropped out of sight, and it later developed that he emigrated from the country at this time.[59] Douglas, too, left London for good, although he was not a missionary and had no official excuse.

The most intense reaction to the *de facto* withdrawal of the Birmingham deputies came from the national rent committee and the members of the union, and it was with them that the deputies clashed most openly. After the Birmingham representatives had left for the convention early in February, leadership within the council had fallen into the hands of several of the more radical men, particularly Emes, now over seventy years of age and increasingly a follower of O'Connor, and William Blaxland, a draper and a man of unusually violent temperament. The moderates on the council quit coming, despite the efforts of Watson and Baker to mediate between the two camps, and by March there was difficulty in getting a quorum; membership in the union dropped off proportionately, until there remained only about one-third of the former subscribers.[60] Under these circumstances the national rent committee easily grew in authority, and soon it conducted meetings of the members nightly in the Bull Ring market next to the working-class district. These nightly meetings regularly attracted four or five hundred people and were harangued in the most unbridled fashion by Brown and other leaders of the rent committee.[61] It was inevitable, of course, that the new leaders would strongly oppose Salt when he made his defeatist speeches to the women's union and to the council on February 18 and 19. Immediately the committee summoned Collins from London to contradict the lampmaker, and it denounced all of its old commanders in the most vigorous terms.[62]

The Birmingham deputies could not well ignore the challenge. In a lead article on March 9, 1839, Douglas observed that the national rent committee had attended to everything but the national rent and that not a sixpence had been received through its efforts. If the members of the union preferred other leadership, he said, let them effect the transference of power "decently, and in order." The following Tuesday at the council session he, Salt, and Hadley demanded an accounting of the money spent by the committee, and when Brown attempted a defense they left without listening to him. The next week, on the 19th, the moderate majority on the council assembled and passed a resolution dissolving the national rent committee, even though they themselves had not chosen the body and it was not directly responsible to them. Much bitterness marked the session. Douglas was hissed by the gallery and he announced that he intended to resign from the council; the spokesmen for the rent committee charged that the Birmingham deputies and the council had deserted the people's cause; and Salt and Hadley complained of the "unmanly whisperings" among the members and declared that the missionaries of the convention could not carry out the assignments given them. Salt asserted that if he had known the difficulties involved in rousing the masses he would have hesitated to have ventured forth at all.[63]

Both the final dissolution of the union and the formal withdrawal of the Birmingham deputies from the convention were at hand. On March 16 the O'Connorites in the convention held a meeting at the Crown and Anchor and talked strongly of physical force; two days later at a dinner at the White Conduit House they repeated their threats. On both occasions there were stern declarations that waverers would be treated as enemies, a clear admonition to the Birmingham deputies.[64] The following week, on March 26, the council of the union met privately in the afternoon, summoned by a circular issued by their old leaders, and the moderate majority determined to call a general meeting of the members and to resign. The deputies among them, excepting Collins, declared that they intended also to resign from the convention. The members were informed of both decisions that evening in a stormy, open session of the council, a meeting that the moderates finally terminated by turning out the lights.[65] Two days later Salt, Douglas, and Hadley wrote Lovett, the secretary of the convention, that they could no longer allow their names to remain on the roll of that assembly. The language used at the recent meeting at the Crown and Anchor, they said, left no doubt that the convention had departed from the great rule of peace, law, and order, which had been the guiding principle of the Birmingham union.[66]

The elected leaders of the union could not be prevented from resigning if they wished, but they were not to get off without humiliation. The rent committee held a meeting of the members of the union on April 1 which upbraided the council for their misdeeds, and then it presided over a gathering of the working classes of the city two days later which censured several of the same men for their misdoings as deputies. The latter meeting was honored by the presence of O'Connor and two of his lieutenants.[67] This meeting resolved to replace the three deserters promptly with new deputies, but it was April 22 before the election was held. On that date a small crowd of workers gathered at the Bull Ring and marched in a procession to Holloway Head; several of the marchers carried a long pole festooned with black crepe and crowned with a copy of the *Journal*, and other participants bore a large lump of salt tied with a black ribbon. After hearing appropriate speeches in which the seceders were chastised once more, the meeting chose Brown, Powell, and Donaldson as the new deputies for Birmingham.[68] Thus was accomplished the formal transference of power as far as Birmingham's representation in the convention was concerned.

No such change-over of officeholders ever took place with respect to the council. On April 9, the old leaders of the union held a last session of the council and adjourned *sine die* without calling the general meeting of members which they had proposed. The highlight of this final session was Salt's reading of a letter from Attwood. The president of the society declared anew his conviction that the Birmingham union was the rallying point for the moral energies of the nation, "giving hope and confidence to the friends of liberty and humanity, and striking terror into the hearts of the oppressors of the people." If the members of the union forgot their solemn duty to obey the council—and Attwood instructed Salt here to read to the members that portion of the *Rules and Regulations* containing this pledge—then all was lost. The letter ended with the admonition,

> My dear Salt, be cautious in what you do. "The times are out of joint." Birmingham is the hope of England. Politically and geographically speaking it is the heart of England. Shall this big and powerful heart cease to beat? Shall England lose the benefit of its generous and vital pulsations? I trust not.

But it was a mark of the changed state of politics that the gallery heard the letter with jeers and laughter. Following the adjournment of the council the audience stayed on to listen to the radical spokesmen among them make speeches more in keeping with their altered tastes.[69]

A week or two after the session the new leaders tried to force the council to call a general meeting of the union by invoking the provision in the *Rules and Regulations* whereby one hundred members could petition for it. The aim of the committee was to arrange for an election which would allow them formally to replace the council. But the petition was rejected by the old officers on the ground of insufficient assurance that the signatures on the document were exclusively those of members.[70] In any case, a mere three hundred men had bought tickets of membership in the quarter beginning in April[71] and now hardly anybody remained to be led. The surviving remnant of the organization dissolved into the physical force Chartist movement. Yet there was a consolation: if it was the fate of the deceased union not to receive the final political rites of formal disbandment, it at least had avoided the ignominy of living on in political sin under rude masters who cared not for the moralist theories of the founders.

CHAPTER IX

Aftermath

A PROFOUND DISILLUSIONMENT soon set in among the former leaders of the union, the kind of dejection that perhaps only defeated crusaders can experience. Two of the deputies, Pierce and Hadley, expressed their feelings by emigrating, Pierce going to New Zealand, where he drowned in a boating accident in 1840, and Hadley going to the Albany district of Australia. Both men entrusted to Salt the settlement of their financial affairs in Birmingham, and in June 1839, Pierce was declared bankrupt. Salt could devote little time to businesses other than his own, because he himself was in a precarious financial position following the theft of a large sum of money by an assistant who had managed his lamp factory while he was in London. Another old leader of the union, Felix Luckcock, went bankrupt in 1839 and emigrated to South Africa, where he died the following year. Isaac Aaron already had left for Australia in the fall of 1838. Those who remained behind lapsed into an immobility which found apt expression in Douglas's reply to O'Connell's call for new activity by moderate reformers: *"There is nothing for it but to anchor till the tide turns. By attempting to beat against it, we shall only lose way."*[1]

It took Attwood a little longer to become infected with a thorough pessimism, for he had not been very closely involved in the events leading to the breakup of the union and the withdrawal of the Birmingham deputies from the convention. In his letters to his wife he had referred proudly to the members of the convention as "my faithful shepherds" and in his letter to Salt, read at the final session of the council, he had urged that the Birmingham deputies reflect much before deciding to quit the movement. When the convention approached him in April, renewing its request that he present the national petition to the House of Commons, he saw his chance to assert command. He wrote Mrs. Attwood, "My rugged Battalions are a little restive, but I shall bring them into strict order, or have nothing to do with them."[2] Nevertheless, the best that the banker could do was to extract a vague statement from the deputies on the subject of physical force, and the exchange left him disgruntled and complaining of the convention's lack of respect for him.[3]

A temporary loss of office by the Melbourne government prevented the presentation of the petition until July 12, 1839. Meanwhile the convention moved to Birmingham, riots occurred in the Bull Ring district there, and the deputies subsequently returned to London. By now further drives had raised the signatures reportedly attached to the document to 1,200,000, but, even so, the House of Commons rejected by a vote of 235 to 46 Attwood's motion that it go into committee to consider the demands of the petition. The adverse vote was expected, and it was not this action that embittered Attwood, but rather a manifesto read by Lord John Russell during the debate on the motion. Unknown to Attwood, the deputies in the convention had been induced by O'Connor and O'Brien to sign a manifesto condemning paper money schemes, and Russell used this document in ridiculing the Birmingham M.P.[4] "I was paralysed," Attwood wrote afterward. "I had created the General Convention. It was the offspring of my own brain. . . . At this very moment, *out of my own camp*, a mortal weapon was directed against my heart!" His conclusion was predictable: "I saw that the doom of my country was sealed."[5]

In October 1839 Attwood moved with his family to St. Helier, Jersey. Two months later he resigned his seat in Parliament and was replaced by his old comrade, G. F. Muntz. In his farewell address to the electors of Birmingham, Attwood declared that "the irresistible moral tempest" he had created had now been converted into hopeless and feeble exhibitions of physical force.

Not only this, but there now was little chance of currency reform on either side of the Atlantic.

> What is this madness in the two foremost nations of the earth? Is it the mere effect of human passion blinding the human judgment? Or is it the effect of some mysterious Providence working its awful dispensations among us? My mind is in the dark.[6]

The banker apparently considered emigrating to Canada,[7] but instead he lived on in retirement in Jersey until his death in 1856 from a creeping paralysis. He took little part in politics during the final years of his life.

Further deaths, migrations, and personal misfortunes afflicted the ranks of the former leadership of the union during the years immediately after the dissolution of the organization. William Trow died in 1839 and William Jennings in 1842, both of them still relatively young men, and Joshua Scholefield died at age 70 in 1844. Joseph Russell, the Radical gadfly of the early union, died in 1840. His Radical colleague of those early days, William Pare, was forced by political enemies to resign as superintendent registrar of records in Birmingham in 1840, and two years later he moved to London; afterward he led a varied career as governor of an Owenite community in Hampshire, railway statist in London, and manager of ironworks in Ireland. Edmonds, the third member of the Radical trio active at the formation of the union, fell gravely ill in 1839, but eventually he recovered and went on to serve long years as clerk of the peace in Birmingham. Collins, their successor as chief Radical in the union, was arrested, along with Lovett, Brown, and Fussell, in connection with the Bull Ring riots of July 1839, the initial charges against them being heard by magistrate P. H. Muntz; Collins served a year's imprisonment in Warwick gaol and after his release he reportedly sank into mental and physical debility before his death about 1850. Two other former leaders left Birmingham in 1842, the Rev. T. M. McDonnell being transferred to a mission near Torquay after quarreling with his bishop, and John Giles emigrating to Canada. William Blaxland, who had sought power by cooperating with the radicals in the last days of the union, went bankrupt in 1842 and was little heard of afterward. An indication of the attrition in the ranks of the old leadership was that only twenty-one persons signed a final accounting of the union's books in September 1841, and only eight of the former leaders were mentioned among the persons attending a dinner in January 1842 to commemorate the twelfth anniversary of the founding of the union.[8]

P. H. Muntz, Salt, Douglas, Edmonds, Emes, Betts, G. F. Muntz (who returned to the city in 1842), and several of the lesser lights remained on in Birmingham, but for them the days of moral crusading were over. Minor involvement in the anti–corn law campaign was as far as they went. Some of them undoubtedly were content with the influence they now wielded in municipal affairs, and others were just too tired to undertake anything new—as Betts wrote to Attwood in 1845, "I would wish to be quiet a little before I go."[9] By all accounts the feeling they shared most was that of moral helplessness, a feebleness in the face of great evil which made serious political action meaningless. In the early 1830s everything had gone right and they had regarded themselves as the political masters of Britain, but in 1838 and 1839, as Attwood observed, "every thing went wrong; the *Serpent*, the *Lion*, and the *Lamb* [the symbols of the union], and all the great principles which they involve, were forgotten."[10] By the time he wrote these words the Chartist movement had collapsed, at least as far as efforts to generate a national movement by moral or by class action were concerned. Local political life in a sense had triumphed, for the movement afterward acquired local and regional characteristics and continued sporadically on that basis for several years. Few of the councilmen lived to see democracy come to Britain.[11]

Because of the peculiar nature of political life in the industrial towns in early nineteenth-century Britain, the primary importance of the union ironically does not lie in the successful movement for parliamentary reform in the early 1830s. Despite their claims, the council had relatively little to do with the nature and outcome of the drive for middle-class political power. The aggregate of local activities everywhere achieved success in that movement, and the council from their provincial perspective merely imagined that the union had instigated and directed things. Had the Birmingham union not existed, the movement probably would not have been very different. The weakness of the council's claims was revealed when the union proved impotent after the passage of the reform bill and was caught up in the party politics which quickly developed in the industrial towns.

With respect to the character of Chartism, on the other hand, the council was of much importance, and had the union not existed the history of the first major effort to gain political power for the working classes would have been considerably different. The contribution made by the leaders of the society was of questionable value, to be sure. Their strategy was based upon the myth of the early 1830s and consisted of moralist manifestoes brandished by political Elijahs against latter-day priests of Baal, an attempt to transcend both localism and party politics by national moral action. Much of the effort had little relationship to the realities of either local or party political life in the late 1830s and early 1840s, and thus it was responsible for many of the frustrations of the Chartist movement. Nothing substantial in the drive for democracy was to be accomplished until party politics, so eschewed by the council, had become involved, concomitantly reducing the influence of local traditions and arrangements, and until evidences of self-discipline and self-improvement by the populace had persuaded the middle classes that working men could be trustworthy citizens. The council's laments of defeat accordingly did not mean that democracy was, as they now supposed, unattainable by peaceful means; rather, their failure meant only that the goal could not be obtained by their methods. Attwood and his associates remained poor prophets to the end.

Notes

Notes to Chapter I

1. *Birmingham Journal*, August 4, 1832. Hereafter cited as *Journal*.

2. Attwood to the editor, February 16, 1832, *Leeds Patriot*, February 18, 1832. For a discussion of Attwood's economic views, see Asa Briggs, "Thomas Attwood and the Economic Background of the Birmingham Political Union," *Cambridge Historical Journal*, IX, no. 2 (1948), 190–216, and Frank W. Fetter's introduction to *Selected Economic Writings of Thomas Attwood* (London, 1964). Among the numerous primary sources, perhaps the most informative is the *Report of the Important Discussion at Beardsworth's Repository, Birmingham, August 28 and 29, 1832, between Messrs. T. Attwood and C. Jones and Mr. Cobbett* (Birmingham, 1832). There are also long quotations of materials given in C. M. Wakefield, *Life of Thomas Attwood* (London, 1885).

3. This was Joseph Parkes's description in a letter to E. J. Stanley, November 30, 1839 (copy), Parkes MSS, University College Library, London.

4. *Birmingham Advertiser*, May 17, 1838. Hereafter cited as *Advertiser*. *The Times*, December 25, 1837.

5. *Journal*, June 11, 1831.

6. The letters were dated April 27 and December 14, 1829, and February 8, 1830. They were sent to Wellington personally and were not published until November 1830.

7. Carlos Flick, "Muntz Metal and Ships' Bottoms: The Industrial Career of G. F. Muntz," *Transactions of the Birmingham and Warwickshire Archaeological Society*, vol. 87 (1975), 70–88.

8. For a discussion of the relationship of the economic and social life of the city to its politics, see the chapter on Birmingham in Asa Briggs, *Victorian Cities* (rev. ed., New York, 1970). Also, the same author's *History of Birmingham*, vol. 2 (London, 1952).

9. *Journal*, May 23, 1829.

10. *Report of the Proceedings at the Meeting of the Inhabitants of*

Birmingham, January 25, 1830 (Birmingham, 1830); Edward Corn to Attwood, December 30, 1829, Birmingham Reference Library; *The Birmingham Monthly Argus and Public Censor* (January 1830), p. 301. The early issues of the *Argus* were not numbered. The series of pamphlets noted above are hereafter cited as *Proceedings.*

11. William Redfern, *A Letter to T. Attwood, in Reply to his Speech* (2nd ed., Birmingham, 1829).

12. *Speech of Thomas Attwood at the Town's Meeting in Birmingham, May 8, 1829* (Birmingham, 1829); *Argus* (August 1829), pp. 37–39.

13. A brief sketch of Edmonds as a politician is given in E. Edwards, *Personal Recollections of Birmingham and Birmingham Men* (Birmingham, 1877), pp. 140–154.

14. A sketch of Pare's career is found in the *Dictionary of National Biography (1895), XLIII, 203–204.* See also George Jacob Holyoake, *Sixty Years of an Agitator's Life* (2 vols., London, 1892), I, 40–41.

15. Leaflet, dated December 10, 1829, in the Birmingham Reference Library with a notation on it; *Journal,* December 12, 19, and 26, 1829.

16. *Journal,* January 2 and 16, 1830.

17. Isaac Spooner, Thomas Lee, and J. F. Ledsam to Peel, January 21, 1830, with enclosed handbill, Home Office 52/11; *Journal,* January 23, 1830.

18. *Proceedings, January 25, 1830; Journal,* January 30, 1830. Both versions of the *Proceedings* are in a collection of pamphlets in the British Library.

19. *Authorized Copy of the Resolutions passed at the Meeting at Birmingham, Held on the 25th of January, 1830, together with the Declaration, Rules and Regulations, of the Political Union* (Birmingham, 1830).

20. For an account of this part of the meeting, see Joseph Russell's *Summary Report of the Important Birmingham Town's Meeting, for Reform, January 25, 1830* (Birmingham, 1830).

21. For example, Attwood's antireform statements in a pamphlet in 1817, *Prosperity Restored* (London), pp. 82, 113, 116–126.

NOTES TO CHAPTER II

1. *Journal,* February 6 and 20, 1830; *Proceedings, May 17, 1830.*

2. Attwood to Mrs. Attwood, August 10, 1831 (copy), Wakefield MSS.

3. *Journal,* February 13, 20, and March 6, 1830.

4. Blandford to Attwood, January 29, 1830, *Journal*, February 6, 1830.

5. A copy of the Declaration was given in *Proceedings, May 17, 1830*.

6. *Proceedings, May 17, 1830; Argus*, II, no. 2 (August 1830), 94; *Journal*, May 8, 1830.

7. *Journal*, July 24 and September 18, 1830.

8. Parkes to George Grote, October 26, 1831, British Museum Additional MSS, 35,149, ff. 117-119.

9. *Coventry Observer*, February 18, 1830; O'Connell to Attwood, February 16, 1830, Daniel O'Connell, *Correspondence of Daniel O'Connell, the Liberator* (ed. W. J. Fitzpatrick (2 vols., London, 1888), I, 199.

10. Broadsheet of amended *Objects, Rules, and Regulations of the Birmingham Political Union*, in the B.R.L.

11. Note by Parkes on the inside cover of a bound volume of *Proceedings*, now in the B.R.L. See also the *Argus*, II, no. 7 (January 1831), 444, and the *Journal*, November 5, 1842.

12. Burdett to Attwood, February 19, 1830, *Journal*, February 27, 1830.

13. Jones stated this fact during the general meeting on July 26. The author found references to only nine unions, including one (at Nottingham) that failed.

14. The author discovered references to thirty-three unions by this date, including those in small towns and villages. Hadley estimated the total number at about forty. *Journal*, January 29, 1831.

15. By the spring of 1831 there were unions at Tipton, Coventry, Dudley, Walsall, Bilston, Worcester, Kidderminster, Warwick, and Darlaston. The Worcester Society sought to become a branch of the union at Birmingham, but its founders were advised that this was illegal. *Worcester Herald*, November 26 and December 4, 1830; Francis Hooper to Lord Melbourne, December 10, 1830, H.O. 52/11.

16. *The Times*, January 27, 1830; *Morning Chronicle*, January 27 and 28, 1830.

17. *Argus* (April 1830), pp. 453–454, and (June 1830), p. 561. The short-lived newspaper was named the *Birmingham and Coventry Free Press*; Russell was publisher and R. Shelton Mackenzie (formerly of the *Journal*) was editor.

18. *Cobbett's Weekly Political Register*, LXIX, no. 5 (January 30, 1830), 151.

19. *Journal*, July 17-August 14, 1830; *Argus*, II, no. 3 (September 1830), 121–122.

20. *Proceedings, July 26, 1830*.

21. *Journal*, July 3, 1830.

22. *Journal*, August 21, September 18, and October 2, 1830; *Argus*, II, no. 3 (September 1830), 152.

23. The authorship of the former song is unknown. The latter was

composed by several persons one evening at Attwood's house, with Bosco as the leading contributor. (Hugh Hutton, *Gathered Leaves of Many Seasons* [London, 1858], pp. xii–xiii.) Hutton and Wakefield, *Attwood*, pp. 199–200, confuse this song with one entitled "The Gathering of the Unions," which was written by E. P. Mead and which was sung at the great Newhall Hill meetings. Copies of these songs and others are preserved in the B.R.L. and in the Wakefield MSS.

24. In addition to the *Proceedings, October 11, 1830*, there was a description of the dinner given in the *Argus*, II, no. 5 (November 1830), 225, and in a leaflet by R. Shelton Mackenzie which was sent to the Home Office by Isaac Spooner, October 15, 1830 (H.O. 52/11).

25. *The Sun* (London), November 11, 1830; *Journal*, November 13, 1830.

26. *Journal*, December 4, 1830; *Proceedings, December 13, 1830*.

27. *Journal*, January 29, 1831.

28. *Morning Chronicle*, February 4, 1831.

NOTES TO CHAPTER III

1. *Proceedings, March 7, 1831*.

2. *Midland Representative*, April 30, 1831. Hereafter cited as *Representative*.

3. *Proceedings, May 2, 1831*.

4. *Morning Chronicle*, January 18, 1831; *Argus*, III, no. 1 (February 1831), 61.

5. *Coventry Herald*, July 29, 1831; *Journal*, July 30, 1831.

6. *Proceedings, July 4, 1831*.

7. *Proceedings, May 2, 1831*.

8. *Journal*, September 10, 1831.

9. *Copy of the Memorial Presented to Earl Grey in October* [sic] *1831*, broadsheet in the B.R.L.; *Political Register*, LXXVII, no. 10 (September 8, 1832), 581-582; *Representative*, September 3–October 1, 1831.

10. *Proceedings, October 3, 1831*; Parkes to George Grote, October 4, 1831; Add. MSS 35,149, f. 77; *Representative*, October 8, 1831; "H" to Wellington, October 9, 1831, Arthur Wellesley, Duke of Wellington, *Dispatches, Correspondence, and Memoranda* (ed. by his son, 8 vols., London, 1867–1880), VII, 559; *Aris's Birmingham Gazette*, October 10, 1831. (Hereafter cited as *Gazette*.) Joseph Hamburger, *James Mill and the Art of Revolution* (New Haven, 1963), pp. 132-139, pointed out that the field at Newhall Hill was not nearly large enough to accommodate the large crowds estimated by the council (although the unionists did count the adjacent streets in their calculations) and that the population of the towns of the northern district scarcely exceeded the numbers that were claimed to have come from it.

11. *Hansard's Parliamentary Debates*, Third Series, VII, 1309–1315; *Extract of Important Letters Just Received by Thomas Attwood, Esq.*, leaflet in Wakefield MSS.

12. Bosco Attwood to Mrs. T. Attwood, October 3, 1831 (copy), Wakefield MSS; *Gazette*, October 10, 1831.

13. *Proceedings, October 3, 1831.*

14. Parkes to Grote, October 4, 1831, Add. MSS 35,149, f. 77.

15. *Hansard*, 3rd S., VII, 1119, 1309–1329.

16. Attwood to Mrs. Attwood, October 9, 1831, Wakefield MSS.

17. *Journal*, October 15, 1831.

18. *Representative*, October 15, 1831.

19. *Extract of Important Letters; Hansard*, 3rd S., VIII, 595–646; Russell to William IV, October 18 (copy); William to Russell, October 19, 1831, Add. MSS 38,080, ff. 54–57.

20. *Representative*, October 15, 1831.

21. Place to Parkes, October 13, 1831 (copy), Parkes to Place, October 15, 1831, Add. MSS 35,149, ff. 89–91, 96–97; *Journal*, October 15, 1831.

22. *Morning Chronicle*, October 24, 1831. A few days later Lord Lyttelton, brother-in-law of Althorp, presided at a public dinner at Birmingham attended by the council and reported that *"in his life* he never heard such a cheer as that for ministers after dinner." Lady Lyttelton to Earl Spencer, October 29, 1831, *Correspondence of Sarah Spencer, Lady Lyttelton, 1787–1870*, ed. Mrs. Hugh Wyndham (London, 1912), pp. 265–266.

23. *Morning Chronicle*, November 1, 1831; Hamburger, *Mill and the Art of Revolution*, p. 73; and Michael Brock, *The Great Reform Act* (London, 1973), pp. 250–253.

24. Althorp to Earl Spencer, October 10, 1831, Sir Denis Le Marchant, *Memoir of John Charles, Viscount Althorp, Third Earl Spencer* (London, 1876), p. 355; Parkes to Grote, October 26 and November 28, 1831 (the latter a copy), Add. MSS 35,149, ff. 117–119, 128–129.

25. Attwood to Mrs. Attwood, October 13, 1831, Wakefield MSS.

26. *Proposed Plan for the Organization of the Birmingham Political Union*, broadsheet in the B.R.L.; *Journal*, November 5–19, 1831.

27. Grey to Burdett, November 24, 1831 (copy), Grey MSS, University of Durham. Wellington complicated matters for Grey by writing the king that the Birmingham union had secretly contracted for 6,000 arms and that it had been done with the permission of the government. Grey easily refuted the allegations and was angry over the duke's unconstitutional approach to the king. *Three Early Nineteenth Century Diaries,* ed. A. Aspinall (London, 1952), pp. 155–157; correspondence among Grey, Sir Herbert Taylor, Wellington, and William IV, November 8–24, 1831, Charles, Earl Grey, *The Reform Act, 1832, The Correspondence of Earl Grey with His Majesty King William IV* (2 vols., London, 1867), I, 412–423, and Grey MSS, box 47, file 9. Grey here and afterward maintained that the unions must be dealt with firmly and given no official sanction,

but that their existence should be tolerated until the passage of the reform bill deprived them of middle-class support.

28. Parkes to Althorp, November 13, 1831, Spencer MSS, Althorp, Northamptonshire; Althorp to Parkes, November 18, 1831, Parkes MSS; Althorp to Grey, November 20, 1831, Spencer MSS; Grey to Althorp, November 20, 1831, Jessie K. Buckley, *Joseph Parkes of Birmingham* (London, 1926), pp. 85–86.

29. *Morning Chronicle*, November 25, 1831; *Representative*, November 26, 1831. The *Morning Chronicle* printed an advance notice of the proclamation on the morning of the 22nd and thus may have given the council several hours warning of it before they met. See also Charles Greville, *The Greville Memoirs: A Journal of the Reigns of King George IV and King William IV*, ed. Henry Reeve (2 vols., New York, 1887), II, 24; and Brock, *The Great Reform Act*, pp. 257–259.

30. *Morning Chronicle*, November 12, 22, and 23, 1831; *The Times*, November 23, 1831.

31. *Journal*, November 26–December 17, 1831.

NOTES TO CHAPTER IV

1. *Standard* (London), November 3–5, 1831.

2. Asa Briggs, "The Local Background of Chartism," *Chartist Studies*, ed. Asa Briggs (London, 1960), p. 18; J. R. M. Butler, *The Passing of the Great Reform Bill* (New York, 1914), p. 303.

3. *Journal*, November 5, 1831.

4. Duncannon to Grey, n.d., Grey MSS.

5. The nearest thing to an indirect communication with the union was a letter in April 1832 to Parkes "from a near connexion of a Member of the Government" approving of the idea of a public meeting at Birmingham. *Argus*, VI, no. 4 (October 1833), 213. For an article on the relations between the government and the union, see Henry Ferguson, "The Birmingham Political Union and the Government, 1831–1832," *Victorian Studies*, III, no. 3 (March 1960), 261–276.

6. Althorp to Parkes, November 6, 1831, Parkes MSS.

7. Lady Lyttelton to Earl Spencer, October 29, 1831, Lady Lyttelton, *Correspondence*, pp. 265–266.

8. *The Times*, November 10, 1831; *Journal*, November 12, 1831.

9. *Journal*, October 29 and November 12, 1831.

10. Cobbett first made the charge in the *Political Register*, LXXIV, no. 4 (October 22, 1831), 243–244. For Carlile's attack, see Richard Carlile, *The Prompter*, no. 51 (October 29, 1831), 885–886.

11. Unions had been established during the summer at Leamington, Willenhall, Nuneaton, Kenilworth, and Warwick. During October and afterward they were formed at Lye, Redditch, Halesowen, Bromsgrove,

Oldbury, Hinckley, Rowley Regis, Sedgley, West Bromwich, Wolverhampton, Wednesbury, Studley, Stratford, and Bridgnorth. By May 1832, there were unions also at Brierley Hill, Smethwick, Harborne, Stourbridge, Alcester, Shirley, Cradley, Bedworth, Handsworth, Solihull, Droitwich, and Tettenhall.

12. For accounts of their formation, see the *Leicester Chronicle*, October 22, 1831; *Derby and Chesterfield Reporter*, December 29, 1831; *Nottingham and Newark Mercury*, November 5 and 12, 1831; and *Gloucester Journal*, November 26, 1831.

13. The March 1832 issue is in the B.R.L. No copy of the second number seems to be extant.

14. The presence of McDonnell and Haynes on the council represented a step forward in tolerance for both the Ultra-Tories and the Dissenters of that body. Edmonds, who had opposed McDonnell during the struggle over Catholic emancipation, now declared that a common concern for liberty was all that mattered. Attwood stated that he himself had always approved of equality for Catholics in principle, but that he had regarded the subject as rather unimportant. In addition, there was an incipient anti-Semitism among the Ultra-Tories, although Attwood and Jones explained that they meant by "evil Jews" only the "stock-jobbing interest." By 1837 this prejudice was overcome sufficiently for them to accept a Jew on the council.

15. Parkes to Grote, December 4, 1831, Add. MSS 35,149, f. 130. For a discussion of Wade's politics, see T. H. Lloyd, "Dr. Wade and the Working Class," *Midland History*, II (Fall 1973), 61–83.

16. *Morning Chronicle*, December 2, 1831.

17. *Gazette*, January 23, 1832; *Journal*, January 28, 1832.

18. *Journal*, February 11 and 25, 1832; Attwood to Mrs. Attwood, February 22, 1832 (copy), Wakefield MSS.

19. *Representative*, March 17, 1832.

20. *Representative*, April 14, 1832.

21. *Political Register*, LXXVI, no. 3 (April 21, 1832), 129–145, no. 4 (April 28, 1832), 198–203.

22. *Journal*, April 28, 1832; *Representative*, April 28, 1832.

23. Joseph Russell, *A Report of the Proceedings at the Grand Meeting of the Birmingham Political Union, May 7, 1832* (Birmingham, 1832); *Journal*, May 5, 1832.

24. In addition to the *Proceedings, May 7, 1832*, the meeting was described by Russell (cited above), by the *Representative*, May 12, 1832, and by *The Times*, May 9, 1832.

25. *Standard*, May 11, 1832. The practice was to calculate adult males at one-fourth of the total head count.

26. Joseph Russell, *A Report of the Immense and Instantaneous Meeting Held at Newhall Hill, May 10, 1832* (Birmingham, 1832); *Journal*, May 12, 1832; *Representative*, May 12, 1832; Robert K. Dent, *Old and New Birmingham* (3 vols., Birmingham, 1879–1880), III, 409. The names of the men who signed the statement are given on a broadsheet, dated May 10, 1832, in the B.R.L.

27. *Proceedings, May 10, 1832;* Russell, *Report of the Immense and Instantaneous Meeting, May 10, 1832; Representative,* May 12, 1832; *Journal,* May 12 and 19, 1832.

28. *Morning Chronicle,* May 12, 1832.

29. Add. MSS 27,793, ff. 98–100, 162–163. For a refutation of the claims made by both men, see Buckley, *Parkes,* pp. 195–196, and Ferguson, "The Birmingham Political Union and the Government." Hamburger, *Mill and the Art of Revolution,* pp. 100–101, believed that the talk may have been designed to influence Melbourne, but this is uncertain.

30. Buckley, *Parkes,* p. 103; Hill to Rowland and Matthew Hill, May 14, 1832, Frederic Hill, *An Autobiography of Fifty Years in Times of Reform,* ed. Constance Hill (London, 1894), pp. 90–92; *Coventry Herald,* May 18, 1832; account by Bosco Attwood in the *Journal,* February 11, 1853.

31. *Solemn Declaration, May 14, 1832,* leaflet in the B.R.L.

32. Hill, *Autobiography,* pp. 91–93; *Coventry Herald,* May 18, 1832; *Journal,* May 19, 1832.

33. *Worcester Herald,* May 19, 1832.

34. Parkes to Mrs. Grote, May 18, 1832, Harriet Grote, *The Personal Life of George Grote* (London, 1873), pp. 78–80; *Argus,* V, no. 5 (May 1833), 299.

35. In addition to the *Proceedings, May 16, 1832,* descriptions of the above events were given in a letter from Parkes to Mrs. Grote, cited above; *Journal,* May 19, 1832; *Representative,* May 19, 1832; Hill to Matthew Hill, May 16, 1832, Hill, *Autobiography,* pp. 97–98; and a collection of clippings by E. Edwards in the B.R.L.

36. *Morning Post* (London), May 16, 1832; Charles Greville, *The Greville Memoirs,* ed. Roger Fulford (rev. ed., London, 1963), p. 93.

37. Attwood to Mrs. Attwood, May 18, 1832 (copy), Wakefield MSS.

38. Attwood to Mrs. Attwood, May 19, 1832 (copy), Wakefield MSS.

39. *Three Early Nineteenth Century Diaries, p. 266.*

40. Attwood to Mrs. Attwood, May 26, 1832 (copy), Wakefield MSS. A full account of the above events was given in *The Times,* May 24, 1832, and the *Journal,* May 26, 1832.

41. Attwood to Mrs. Attwood, May 19, 1832 (copy), Wakefield MSS. See also the statements by Attwood in the *Proceedings, May 28, 1832* (in which he gave the figure as "seven or eight hundred thousand"), and by Bosco Attwood in the *Journal,* February 11, 1853.

42. Place to Grote, May 15, 1832, Place to Hobhouse, May 8, 1832 (copies), Add. MSS 35,149, ff. 144, 150. Place wrote later that he, Attwood, Scholefield, and Parkes had agreed upon a run on the banks, to be led by the National Political Union and followed up by the Birmingham Union, but there is no evidence to support the assertion and much reason to doubt it. Add. MSS 27,819, ff. 101–102. For an account

of Place's activity in this respect, see Hamburger, *Mill and the Art of Revolution*, pp. 102–106, and Carlos Flick, "Thomas Attwood, Francis Place, and the Agitation for British Parliamentary Reform," *Huntington Library Quarterly*, XXXIV, no. 4 (August 1971), 355–366.

43. Wade to Attwood, November 12, 1832, *True Sun* (London), November 14, 1832; *Argus*, IV, no. 2 (July 1832), 122.

44. Attwood to Mrs. Attwood, May 19 and 26, 1832 (copies), Wakefield MSS.

NOTES TO CHAPTER V

1. Attwood to Mrs. Attwood, May 23, 1832 (copy), Wakefield MSS.

2. The writers were Thomas Clark and E. Edwards. Both items are part of a collection of clippings by the latter in the B.R.L.

3. *Proceedings, May 28, 1832*.

4. B.R. Haydon, *The Diary of Benjamin Robert Haydon* (5 vols., Cambridge, Mass., 1963), III, 620–621.

5. Leaflet, dated June 29, 1832, in Wakefield MSS.

6. *Political Register*, LXXVI, no. 11 (June 16, 1832), 650–651, 679, 683; *Journal*, June 16 and 23, 1832; *Proceedings, June 25, 1832*.

7. *Proceedings, July 26, 1830; Journal*, July 9, 1831; *Argus*, IV, no. 3 (August 1832), 207–208.

8. Parkes to Place, May 2, 1832, Add. MSS 27,792 f. 306.

9. *Journal*, May 20, 1837.

10. *Speech of Thomas Attwood on the State of the Country, March 21, 1833* (London, 1833), p. 19; *Morning Chronicle*, May 22, 1832; *Argus*, III, no. 7 (August 1831), 235.

11. *Argus, IV, no. 1 (June 1832)*, 72.

12. Circular, dated June 12, 1832, in the B.R.L.; *Journal*, June 16–July 28, 1832; Joseph Russell, *The Substance of the Extraordinary Proceedings at the Birmingham Political Council, on Tuesday Evening, July 3, on the Subject of Pledges* (Birmingham, 1832).

13. Leaflet, dated July 25, 1832, in the B.R.L.; *Journal*, July 21 and 28, 1832.

14. *Proceedings, July 30, 1832; Journal*, August 25, 1832.

15. Althorp to Attwood, July 15, 1832, Attwood to Mrs. Attwood, August 2 and September 2, 1832 (copies), Wakefield MSS.

16. *Report of Discussion at Beardsworth's Repository, August 28 and 29, 1832*. Cobbett also published his version of the debate, entitled *Mansell and Co.'s Report*.

17. Grey to Attwood, September 5, 1832 (copy), Wakefield MSS.

18. *Political Register*, LXXVI, no. 9 (June 2, 1832), 531.

19. *Hull Advertiser*, September 7, 1832.

20. *Journal*, July 14 and 21, 1832.

21. *Journal*, March 15, 1834.

22. Parkes to Place, January 17, 1833, Add. MSS 35,149, ff. 210–211.

23. *Journal,* November 10, 1832.

24. *Journal,* January 5, 26, and February 2, 1833.

25. Leaflet, dated February 19, 1833, in the B.R.L.; *Journal,* February 9 and 23, 1833.

26. *Journal,* March 2, 1833; *Gazette,* March 4, 1833.

27. *Manchester Guardian,* January 19, 1833.

28. Western to Attwood, January 21, 1833; Attwood to Bosco Attwood, February 9, 1833 (copies), Wakefield MSS.

29. *Hansard,* 3rd S., XVI, 918–938, 961–962.

30. *Morning Chronicle,* March 22, 1833; *Examiner,* March 24, 1833; *The Times,* March 22, 23, 28, and April 1, 1833. Attwood's letter was dated March 28.

31. *Journal,* March 30, April 13 and 27, 1833.

32. *Journal,* May 4, 1833.

33. During the May 1832 crisis new unions had been formed at Astwood Bank, Stourport, Grand Junction, Hanley, Cannock, Coseley, Bloxedge, and Henley-in-Arden, raising the total to about fifty.

34. Leaflet, dated May 9, 1833, in the B.R.L.; *Journal,* May 11, 1833.

35. Attwood to Mrs. Attwood, May 18, 1833 (copy), Wakefield MSS.

36. *Proceedings, May 20, 1833; The Times,* May 21–24, 1833; *Gazette,* May 27, 1833.

37. *Manchester Guardian,* May 25, 1833; *Leeds Mercury,* May 25, 1833.

38. *Journal,* May 25–June 15, 1833; *Gazette,* May 27 and June 10, 1833.

39. *Journal,* June 29, 1833.

40. *Proceedings, September 16, 1833.*

41. *Advertiser,* November 28, 1833.

42. *Advertiser,* December 26, 1833; *Journal,* February 22, 1834.

43. *Argus,* VII, no. 3 (March 1834), 149, 153, and 198.

44. *Journal,* June 7, 1834.

45. *Leeds Mercury,* June 21, 1834.

NOTES TO CHAPTER VI

3. *Proceedings, September 15, 1834; Journal,* September 20 and 27, 1834.

4. Attwood to Mrs. Attwood, November 19 and 24, 1834 (copies), Wakefield MSS; *Proceedings, November 28, 1834.*

5. *Proceedings, August 18, 1835.*
6. *Proceedings, September 4, 1835.*
7. *Journal*, August 13 and 20, 1836.
8. The alignment of voters in elections for local offices in 1837 was roughly 1,000 Conservatives, 1,000 Dissenters and reformist Whigs, 300 old-line Whigs, 2,000 Ultra-Tory and Radical unionists, and 500 uncommitted. By including some Liberals on their lists the unionists easily carried the elections. *Journal*, November 10, 1838.
9. *Proceedings, January 18, 1836.*
10. *Morning Chronicle*, March 6, 1833.
11. *Journal*, April 15, 1837. The letter was not dated.
12. Attwood to Mrs. Attwood, May 26, 1837 (copy), Wakefield MSS.
13. *Journal*, April 22 and May 27, 1837.
14. Leaflet, dated May 10, 1837, and pamphlet, undated, in the B.R.L.; *Advertiser*, May 25, 1837.
15. McDonnell to John Lalor, January 2, 1837, *The Times*, February 6, 1837; Attwood to Mrs. Attwood, May 16, 1837 (copy), Wakefield MSS.
16. *Hansard*, 3rd S., XXXVIII, 1189–1205, 1208; *The Times*, June 6, 1837.
17. Attwood to P.H. Muntz, June 6, 1837, *Journal*, June 10, 1837.
18. T.A. Attwood to Mrs. Attwood, May 14, 1833 (copy), Wakefield MSS.
19. *Advertiser*, June 8, 1837; *Journal*, June 10, 1837.
20. *Journal*, June 3 and 10, 1837.
21. *Advertiser*, June 22, 1837; *Philanthropist* (Birmingham), June 22, 1837; *Journal*, June 24, 1837. For a discussion of the origin of the idea of a "sacred holiday," see Iorwerth Prothero, "William Benbow and the Concept of the 'General Strike', " *Past and Present*, no. 63 (May 1974), 132–171.
22. *Journal*, July 15, 1837.
23. *Advertiser*, June 29, 1837; *Journal*, July 1 and 8, 1837.
24. *Gazette*, August 13, 1838.
25. Attwood to Mrs. Attwood, November 23, 28, and December 1, 1837 (copies), Wakefield MSS; *Journal*, October 7, November 4 and 11, 1837.
26. Parkes to E.J. Stanley, September 24, 1837 (copy), Parkes MSS; *Journal*, June 10, 1837.
27. *Journal*, October 21 and 28, 1837.
28. *Gazette*, December 11, 1837. The address was dated December 7.
29. *Journal*, November 11, 1837; *Philanthropist*, December 28, 1837.
30. *Journal*, December 2, 1837; *Gazette*, December 11, 1837.
31. L.W.M.A. Minute Book, December 11, 1837, Add. MSS

37,773, f. 83; *Journal*, December 16, 1837; *Weekly True Sun*, December 17, 1837.

32. *Gazette*, December 18, 1837; *The Times*, December 25, 1837.

NOTES TO CHAPTER VII

1. *Journal*, January 20, 1838.

2. *Journal*, December 30, 1837.

3. *Journal*, January 20 and February 24, 1838; *Philanthropist*, February 22, 1838.

4. *Coventry Herald*, January 5, 1838.

5. The union was entitled "The Midland Union of the Working Classes." It was formed on October 29, 1832, and lasted about four months.

6. *Journal*, January 13, 1838.

7. Place to Hume, February 10, 1840 (copy), Add. MSS 35,151, f. 207. For an account of the formation of the London Working Men's Association, see J.T. Ward, *Chartism* (New York, 1973), pp. 70–75.

8. *Journal*, February 24, March 10 and 31, 1838.

9. L.W.M.A. Minute Book, May 31, June 6 and 7, December 5, 1837, and March 27, 1838, Add. MSS 37,773, ff. 51–55, 82, 101. For a discussion of the authorship of the Charter, see D.J. Rowe, "The London Working Men's Association and the 'People's Charter', " *Past and Present*, no. 36 (April 1967), pp. 81–85.

10. *Northern Star* (Leeds), January 6, 1838; *Journal*, February 3, 1838.

11. *Journal*, March 3, 1838.

12. *The Times*, December 5, 1837. Salt later testified that the idea of the convention originated with either P.H. Muntz or Attwood; but there is no evidence for the latter. *The Trial of W. Lovett for a Seditious Libel, August 6, 1839* (2nd ed., London, 1839), pp. 7–8.

13. *Journal*, February 24 and March 3, 1838. Place incorrectly identified Collins as a shoemaker (Add. MSS 27,820, f. 78) and this error has been repeated by many writers.

14. *Philanthropist*, February 8, 1838; Salt to Ebenezer Elliott, April 16, 1838, *Sheffield Iris*, May 1, 1838.

15. *Cheltenham Chronicle*, December 27, 1838.

16. *Scotch Reformers' Gazette* (Glasgow), April 14–28, 1838; Purdie to Attwood, April 25, 1838, Wakefield, *Attwood*, pp. 333–334.

17. *The Scotsman* (Edinburgh), May 9 and 16, 1838; *Journal*, May 19, 1838.

18. *Journal*, May 5–19, 1838. There is no basis for Place's claim that the committee failed to report to the full council because they wanted to avoid discussion to hide the fact that the petition really was a

191

clever argument for the cause of cheap currency. (Add. MSS 27,820, ff. 96–97, 131–132.) There was in fact only one passing reference to currency in the document. For a leaflet edition of the petition, see the Lovett Collection in the B.R.L., I, 297.

19. *Glasgow Courier*, April 28, 1838; *The Scotsman*, May 9, 1838.

20. L.W.M.A. Minute Book, May 1, 8, and 22, 1838, Add. MSS 37,773, ff. 105–107. A pamphlet copy of *The People's Charter* is in the British Library.

21. L.W.M.A. Minute Book, May 15, 1838, Add. MSS 37,773, f. 106; Lovett to W. Sharman Crawford [June 3 or 4, 1838] (copy), Lovett Collection, I, 170.

22. Add. MSS 27,820, f. 137; *Journal*, June 9, 1838.

23. *Advertiser*, May 17, 1838; *Journal*, May 19, 1838.

24. Attwood to Mrs. Attwood, May 18 and 20, 1838 (copies), Wakefield MSS; *Journal*, May 26, 1838, and March 30, 1839.

25. Accounts of the proceedings were given in the *Glasgow Courier*, May 22, 1838, and the *Scotch Reformers' Gazette*, May 26, 1838, as well as the *Journal*, May 26, 1838. See also Alexander Wilson, *The Chartist Movement in Scotland* (New York, 1970), pp. 47–51.

26. Attwood to Mrs. Attwood, May 21, 22, and 23, 1838 (copies), Wakefield MSS; *The Scotsman*, May 30, 1838; *Journal*, May 26, June 2 and 16, 1838.

27. *The News* (London), July 8, 1838. Attwood's letter was dated July 6.

28. *Journal*, March 31 and June 2, 1838; *Northern Liberator* (Newcastle), June 2, 1838.

29. L.W.M.A. Minute Book, May 22, 29, and June 12, 1838, Add. MSS 37,773, ff. 107–109; Lovett to members of the "Birmingham Council," n.d. (copy), Lovett Collection, I, 174.

30. *Journal*, June 9, 1838.

31. L.W.M.A. Minute Book, June 19 and 28, 1838, Add. MSS 37,773, ff. 110–111; *Journal*, June 23, 1838.

32. Lovett to Salt, n.d. (copy), Douglas to Lovett, July 17, 1838, Lovett Collection, I, 180, 208.

33. *Northern Star*, April 28 and May 5, 1838.

34. *Manchester Guardian*, June 6, 1838; *Northern Liberator*, June 9, 1838; *Manchester Advertiser*, June 9, 1838.

35. *Northern Star*, June 9, 1838; *Journal*, June 9 and 16, 1838.

36. *Manchester Advertiser*, June 9, 1838; *Journal*, June 16, 1838. For a discussion of O'Connor's and other Northerners' use of the language of violence, see Thomas Milton Kemnitz, "Approaches to the Chartist Movement: Feargus O'Connor and Chartist Strategy," *Albion*, V (Spring, 1973), 67–73; and William Henry Maehl, Jr., "The Dynamics of Violence in Chartism: A Case Study in Northeastern England," *Albion*, VII *(Summer, 1975)*, 101–119.

37. *Northern Star*, June 9, 1838.

38. *Northern Star*, June 16, 1838; *Journal*, June 30, 1838.

39. *Journal*, July 28, 1838.

NOTES TO CHAPTER VIII

1. Attwood to Mrs. Attwood, July 14 and 17, 1838 (copies), Wakefield MSS.

2. *Journal*, July 28 and August 4, 1838; *Advertiser*, August 9, 1838; T.C. Salt, *To the Women of Birmingham*, August 16, 1838, leaflet in the B.R.L.

3. Salt to Thomas Devyr, June 27, 1838, *Northern Liberator*, June 30, 1838; *Journal*, July 28 and August 4, 1838.

4. Attwood to Mrs. Attwood, August 3, 1838 (copy), Wakefield MSS.

5. Salt to Lovett, postmarked March 8, 1839, Add. MSS 34,245A, ff. 107–110; *Journal*, February 23 and March 23, 1839.

6. *Journal*, August 25, 1838; *Northern Star*, September 21, 1839.

7. *Proceedings, August 6, 1838; Advertiser*, August 9, 1838; *Northern Star*, August 11, 1838; *Gazette*, August 13, 1838.

8. Attwood to Mrs. Attwood, August 7, 1838 (copy), Wakefield MSS.

9. *Proceedings, August 6, 1838; Morning Advertiser* (London), August 7, 1838.

10. *Journal*, February 24 and August 18, 1838.

11. *Journal*, August 25 and November 10, 1838.

12. *Journal*, September 29, 1838.

13. Douglas to Lovett, September 12, 1838, Lovett Collection, I, 234; *Morning Advertiser*, September 18, 1838.

14. *The Times*, September 24, 1838; *Manchester Guardian*, September 26, 1838; *Manchester Advertiser*, September 29, 1838.

15. *Liverpool Mercury*, September 28, 1838; *Liverpool Chronicle*, September 29, 1838.

16. *Northern Star*, October 16, 1838; *Bradford Observer*, October 18, 1838.

17. *Journal*, September 22–October 20, 1838.

18. T.P. Thompson to Place, September 18, 1838, Add. MSS 35,151, f. 96; *Journal*, September 22, 1838.

19. For a description of Chartism in the Southwest, see R.B. Pugh, "Chartism in Somerset and Wiltshire," *Chartist Studies*, pp. 174–219.

20. In addition to the sources cited in notes 14 and 15, see the *Northern Star*, September 29, 1838 and the *Journal*, September 29, 1838.

21. *The Times*, October 18, 1838.

22. *Northern Star*, September 1, 1838; *Journal*, September 1, 1838; *Staffordshire Examiner* (Wolverhampton), November 17 and 24, 1838.

23. *Coventry Herald*, September 7, 1838; *Northern Star*, September 8, 1838; *Journal*, October 20, 1838.

24. Salt to Lovett, postmarked March 8, 1839, Add. MSS 34,245A, ff. 107–110; *Journal*, March 23, 1839.

25. *Sheffield Iris*, September 25 and October 2, 1838; *Nottingham*

Review, November 9, 1838; *Leicestershire, Nottinghamshire, and Derbyshire Telegraph* (Loughborough), November 10, 1838; *Staffordshire Advertiser* (Stafford), November 17, 1838; *Leicester Chronicle,* November 24, 1838.

26. *Operative,* February 10, 1839.

27. Salt to Lovett, October 26, 1838, Lovett Collection, I, 286.

28. *Proceedings, August 6, 1838.*

29. *Coventry Herald,* September 7, 1838; *Journal,* September 1 and 7, 1838.

30. *Northern Star,* October 27, 1838; *Operative,* November 4, 1838.

31. *Journal,* October 27, 1838.

32. *Journal,* May 5, 1838.

33. *Journal,* November 3 and 10, 1838; *Northern Star,* November 17, 1838.

34. *Northern Star,* November 17, 1838; *Journal,* November 17, 1838.

35. *Journal,* November 17 and 24, 1838. Attwood's letter was dated November 15.

36. *Leicester Chronicle,* November 24, 1838.

37. *Northern Star,* November 24 and December 1, 1838; *Journal,* November 24 and December 1, 1838; *Advertiser,* December 13, 1838.

38. Douglas to Lovett, February 16, 1839, Add. MSS 34,245A, f. 38. A good contemporary sketch of Salt appeared in *The Charter* (London), March 3, 1839.

39. *Advertiser,* March 7, 1839.

40. *Journal,* December 29, 1838; *Advertiser,* January 3, 1839.

41. Parkes to E. J. Stanley, December 27, 1838 (copy), Parkes MSS.

42. *Cheltenham Free Press,* December 29, 1838; *Bristol Gazette,* December 27, 1838; *Reading Mercury,* January 19, 1839; *Journal,* January 19, 1839.

43. *Journal,* December 22, 1838, January 19 and 26, 1839.

44. L.W.M.A. Minute Book, December 13, 1838, Add. MSS 37,773, f. 133.

45. *Sun,* December 19–21, 29, 1838; *Northern Star,* December 22 and 29, 1838; Add. MSS 27,820, ff. 353–358.

46. *Northern Star,* January 12 and 19, 1839; *Northern Liberator,* January 19, 1839.

47. *Northern Star,* February 2, 1839; *Operative,* February 10, 1839.

48. Attwood to Mrs. Attwood, February 4, 1839 (copy), Wakefield MSS.

49. *Northern Star,* December 29, 1838, and January 19, 1839.

50. Douglas to Lovett, January 29, 1839, Lovett Collection, I, 297; *Journal,* February 2, 1839.

51. *Operative,* February 10, 1839.

52. *Advertiser*, February 7, 1839; *Journal*, February 9, 1839.

53. *Charter*, February 10, 1839; *Operative*, February 10, 1839.

54. *Northern Star*, February 16, 1839; *Charter*, February 17, 1839; *Operative*, February 17, 1839.

55. Douglas and Salt to Lovett, February 17, 1839, Add. MSS 34,245A, ff. 41–42; *Journal*, February 23, 1839.

56. *Northern Star*, February 23, 1839; *Charter*, February 24, 1839; *Operative*, February 24, 1839; *Manchester Advertiser*, March 9, 1839.

57. For example, Peter Bussey's interview with Salt as reported in the *Bradford Observer*, March 7, 1839.

58. Collins to Lovett, March 17, 1839, Add. MSS 34,245A, f. 136; *Journal*, March 16 and 23, 1839.

59. Salt to Lovett, postmarked March 8, 1839, Add. MSS 34,245A, ff. 107–110; *Advertiser*, March 14, 1839.

60. P. H. Muntz to the editor, May 22 and June 5, 1839, *Northern Star*, June 1 and 8, 1839.

61. W. Dugdale to Lord John Russell, March 27, 1839, J. Lawrence to Russell, April 30, 1839, H.O. 40/50/15–22.

62. *Journal*, March 2, 1839.

63. *Journal*, March 16 and 23, 1839; *Advertiser*, April 4, 1839.

64. *Morning Chronicle*, March 19, 1839.

65. *Advertiser*, March 28 and April 4, 1839; *Journal*, March 30, 1839.

66. Hadley, Douglas, and Salt to Lovett, March 28, 1839, Add. MSS 34,245A, f. 175.

67. *Advertiser*, April 4, 1839.

68. *Advertiser*, April 25, 1839.

69. *Journal*, April 13, 1839. Attwood's letter was dated March 28.

70. *Journal*, June 1, 1839.

71. P. H. Muntz to the editor, May 22 and June 5, 1839, Henry Hawkes to P. H. Muntz, May 27, 1839, *Northern Star*, June 1 and 8, 1839.

Notes to Chapter IX

1. *Journal*, June 1, 1839.

2. Attwood to Mrs. Attwood, May 1, 1839 (copy), Wakefield MSS.

3. MS note quoted in Wakefield, *Attwood*, pp. 344–345.

4. *Hansard*, 3rd S., XLIX, 220–278.

5. Attwood to the Peace, Law, and Order Society, and to all the Inhabitants of Birmingham, July 17, 1839, *Journal*, July 20, 1839.

6. Leaflet, dated December 9, 1839, Add. MSS 27,821, f. 317.

7. Wakefield, *Attwood*, p. 380.

8. *Journal*, September 25, 1841, and February 5, 1842.

9. Betts to Attwood, December 15, 1845 (copy), Wakefield MSS.

10. *Journal*, June 19, 1841. In this issue of the *Journal* and in those of June 26 and July 17 Attwood offered a brief sketch of the union's involvement in the Chartist movement, but he never developed it further. The Birmingham leaders, unlike the Chartist chieftains elsewhere, were too disillusioned to record their activities in memoirs and autobiographies.

11. The principal exception was P. H. Muntz, who in his old age was elected to Parliament in 1868 as a Liberal to fill the third seat given to Birmingham by the Reform Bill of 1867.

Bibliographical Note

The official records of the Birmingham Political Union have disappeared, but inevitably the society, believing as it did that publicity was the very essence of politics, left behind a large deposit of printed materials. Through a careful sifting of these materials, augmented by manuscript and other sources, a relatively complete chronicle of the union's activities can be constructed.

The principal source for the internal business of the union, consisting mainly of the deliberations of the council of the society, is the *Birmingham Journal*. The editor in 1830-1831 was a High Tory named Jonathan Crowther, and after some initial quarrels with Thomas Attwood and others he had his reporters attend the sessions of the council regularly and report them fully. In 1832, after his relationship with the unionists had cooled, new owners of the *Journal* replaced him as editor with William Greatheed Lewis, a former reporter for one of the London dailies. Lewis resumed the weekly reports of the sittings of the council and continued them through the summer of 1833, after which the sessions and information on them in the press became irregular, presaging the demise of the union in 1834. When the society was revived in 1837 the *Journal* was being edited by Robert K. Douglas, who came to Birmingham from Dumfries. Douglas served as one of the leaders of the union and so reported the council's debates and business with some bias but in considerable detail until the second collapse of the union in 1839.

These reports in the *Journal* are rendered more valuable still by the presence in other newspapers of accounts with which the *Journal's* version can be compared. During the period of the agitation for the reform bill the newspaper with the largest circulation in Birmingham, *Aris's Birmingham Gazette*, was edited by Thomas Knott, a Tory. Knott took little interest in the daily affairs of the union, but he set as his task the correction of "misrepresentations" made by the *Journal*, and occasionally he had his reporters attend the meetings of the council for that purpose. The same function was performed in 1831 and 1832 from a radical perspective by the *Midland Representative*, edited by James Bronterre O'Brien. Although O'Brien looked upon the union more favorably than did the editor of the *Gazette*, he was quick to censure its leaders when they "erred." In addition, there was published in Birmingham until 1834 a monthly journal entitled *The Birmingham Monthly Argus and Public Censor*, a scandal sheet written and published by an Ultra-Tory opponent of Attwood named Joseph Allday. The *Argus* delighted in printing unfavorable revelations about the union and its leaders, supplied to Allday by dissident members, and probably provided also by the editor's brother, who was a member of the council. After the union was revived in 1837 the most effective criticism came from the *Birmingham Advertiser*, a Conservative newspaper edited by Jonathan Crowther, the union's old friend now turned enemy. From his *Journal* days Crowther had inside knowledge of the union and of its chieftains, and he sought to expose what he believed to be their foibles and false claims. Finally, another major political group in Birmingham, the Dissenters, published a newspaper from 1835 to 1838 entitled *The Reformer*, later renamed *The Philanthropist*. Its editor was Joseph Shearman, a surgeon, and under his guidance it covered the revived union's affairs closely and fairly and thus provides a relatively unbiased account of them.

The major sources for the official business of the union, consisting of addresses and proclamations to the union members and to the public, are the collections of unionist leaflets and broadsheets in the Birmingham Reference Library and the British Library. In addition, many items of business were advertised in the Birmingham and London press. Accounts of the public meetings of the union were given in pamphlet *Proceedings* printed and distributed by the *Journal*. Almost complete collections of these pamphlets are preserved in the Birmingham Reference Library and the British Library, occasionally in more than one edition and therefore inviting comparison. The lawyer Joseph Parkes is reported to have censored the pamphlets before they were printed, and thus it is well that there are available other accounts of the most important meetings. An independent set of *Proceedings* of several of the great meetings was published by Joseph Russell, a Radical who participated in the founding of the union but who later left it, and on several occasions both *The Times* and the *Coventry Herald* sent their own reporters to Birmingham. Also, the other newspapers at Birmingham gave their own observations on the meetings, and there were a few reports sent to the Home Office by the magistrates and others in Birmingham, reports now in the Public Record Office.

The private and political papers of all of the principal leaders of the union have been lost. Fortunately, C. M. Wakefield, the official biographer of Attwood (*Life of Thomas Attwood* [London, 1885]), had access to the founder's private papers and he made copies of them in a ledger. The ledger, along with a few letters, is in the possession of Wakefield's descendant, Mrs. Geoffrey Williams, of London. Of the other leaders, only the papers of George F. Muntz seem to have survived, and these manuscripts, in the possession of the industrialist's great-grandson, Mr. F. D. Muntz of Henley-in-Arden, contain only business and legal records. The disappearance of the political correspondence of Attwood and others, however, is offset partially by the presence in the *Journal* of the text of important letters sent to Attwood as chairman of the union, letters which apparently were published because of the council's policy of keeping all such matters open and legal.

The scattered state of the sources perhaps explains why there has been little published by historians on the subject of the union and its chieftains. Only one article has appeared on the activities of the union: Henry Ferguson, "The Birmingham Political Union and the Government, 1831-1832," *Victorian Studies*, III, no. 3 (March 1960), 261-276. On Attwood himself, in addition to Wakefield's biography, there have appeared articles by Asa Briggs, "Thomas Attwood and the Economic Background of the Birmingham Political Union," *Cambridge Historical Journal*, IX, no. 2 (1948), 190-216; by Carlos Flick, "Thomas Attwood, Francis Place, and the Agitation for British Parliamentary Reform," *Hun-*

tington Library Quarterly, XXXIV, no. 4 (August 1971), 355-366; and an introduction by Frank W. Fetter to *Selected Economic Writings of Thomas Attwood* (London, 1964). With regard to the other leaders of the union, there is an article by Carlos Flick on G. F. Muntz as an industrialist, "Muntz Metal and Ships' Bottoms: The Industrial Career of G. F. Muntz," *Transactions of the Birmingham and Warwickshire Archeological Society,* LXXXVII (1975), 70-88; and one on Dr. Arthur Wade by T. H. Lloyd, "Dr. Wade and the Working Class," *Midland History,* II (Fall, 1973), 61-83. Otherwise, the leading unionists remain relatively unknown, without authors.

The most useful primary sources relating to persons and organizations that had connections with the union and its leaders are the Parkes MSS in the University College Library, London; the Place MSS and the minute books of the London Working Men's Association in the British Museum; and the Lovett Collection in the Birmingham Reference Library. The papers of the leaders of the government contain little of direct interest on the subject of the union, but they are important in a negative sense in that they substantiate other evidence that the union played mostly a local role in the agitation for the reform bill. The papers canvassed by the author are the Grey MSS, Prior's Kitchen, University of Durham; the Spencer MSS, Althorp, Northamptonshire; the Durham MSS, Biddick Hall, County Durham; the Graham MSS (microfilm), Cambridge University Library; the Brougham MSS, University College Library; the Russell MSS, British Museum and Public Record Office; the Holland House MSS, British Museum; and the Broughton MSS, British Museum. Few of the numerous volumes of published memoirs and correspondence by the above leaders and lesser figures of the day contain material relating to the union, although they are excellent for the general politics of the period.

For the political activities of the Tory and Whig leaders during the reform bill period the author has relied chiefly upon research conducted for his doctoral thesis. The reader, however, is referred to the excellent recent survey of the government's actions given in Michael Brock, *The Great Reform Act* (London, 1973). For the Chartist agitation, the two best general works are J. T. Ward, *Chartism* (New York, 1973), and Asa Briggs, ed.,

Chartist Studies (London, 1960). The Birmingham background of the union is best surveyed in the book by Asa Briggs, *History of Birmingham,* vol. II (London, 1952), in the chapter on Birmingham in his *Victorian Cities* (rev. ed., New York, 1970), and in an article by him, "The Background of the Parliamentary Reform Movement in Three English Cities (1830-1832)," *Cambridge Historical Journal,* X, no. 3 (1952); 293-317. Also, there are three works published by nineteenth-century writers which are useful on the local background of the union: E. Edwards, *Personal Recollections of Birmingham and Birmingham Men* (Birmingham, 1877); Robert K. Dent, *Old and New Birmingham* (3 vols., Birmingham, 1879-1880); and Frederic Hill, *An Autobiography of Fifty Years in Times of Reform,* ed. Constance Hill (London, 1894). The best grasp of the varied activities of the city during the second quarter of the nineteenth century, however, is to be obtained from a reading of the half-dozen newspapers printed in Birmingham during the period.

Index

Aaron, Isaac, 119, 175

Althorp, Viscount (3rd Earl Spencer), 62, 65-69, 73, 99

Aris's Birmingham Gazette, 46

Attwood, Charles, 86

Attwood, George de Bosco, 41, 62, 89, 104-05, 118, 183 n.23

Attwood, Matthias, 99

Attwood, Thomas, character, 18-19, 43, 58, 67-68, 72-73, 102-03, 135; influence within the union, 57-58, 66, 76, 113-14, 117, 122-23, 135, 164, 174-75; in Parliament, 19, 94, 102, 104-05, 112, 114, 117, 121, 142, 176; retirement and death, 175-76

Baker, Thomas, 128, 152, 166, 171

Barnes, Thomas, 46

Bath Working Men's Association, 131

Betts, John, 34, 163, 178

Bibb, James, 75

Biddle, Joseph, 41, 118

Birmingham and Coventry Free Press, 46

Birmingham Journal, 42, 46, 63, 80, 86, 89, 101, 115-16, 118, 141, 143-44, 150, 157, 160, 170, 173

Birmingham and Midland Reform Association, 113-14, 116, 118

Birmingham Monthly Argus and Public Censor, 97, 110

Birmingham Political Union, formation of, 17-18, 26-28, 33-35; principles of, 28-31; finances of, 37-38, 96-97, 116, 121, 127, 140, 148; enrollment in, 37-38, 40, 52, 76, 81-84, 86, 97, 101, 116-17, 121, 148, 171, 174; membership on the council, 27, 34, 40-41, 57, 75-76, 89, 98, 101-02, 117-19, 152, 163, 171-73; relations with the government, 54-55, 59-60, 62-69, 71-73, 83-86, 89, 100, 104-06, 111, 119, 121-22; relationship with the Established Church, 42, 58, 64, 78, 111-12; relations with other political unions, 29-30, 43-45, 57, 61-62, 65-69, 71-72, 74-75, 79, 84, 106-07, 109, 126-28; May 17, 1830 meeting, 37, 39-40, 44, 47; July 26, 1830 meeting, 44, 47; October 11, 1830 meeting, 48-50; and the fall of Wellington's government, 50-52; October 3, 1831 meeting, 59-63, 79-80; efforts to reorganize, 66-69; May 7, 1832 meeting, 78-81; May 10, 1832 meeting, 82-83; "Solemn Declaration" of, 85-86, 88, 130; June 25, 1832 meeting, 95; agitation by in 1833, 103-08; February 25, 1833 meeting, 104; May 20, 1833 meeting, 106-08; disbandment of in 1833, 108-09;